FORD CORTINA 1600E

Graham Robson

CONTENTS

Foulis

Haynes

ISBN 0 85429 310 8

A FOULIS Motoring Book

First published 1984

Published by:
Haynes Publishing Group
Sparkford, Yeovil,
Somerset BA22 7JJ

Distributed in USA by:
Haynes Publications Inc.
861 Lawrence Drive, Newbury
Park, California 91320, USA

Editor: Mansur Darlington
Dust jacket design: Rowland Smith
Page Layout: Tim Rose
Colour photographs: Courtesy of
Ford of Britain or specially taken
by Andrew Morland
Road tests: Courtesy of Motor,
Autosport and Good Motoring
Printed in England by: J.H.Haynes
& Co. Ltd

Further titles in this series will be published at
regular intervals. For information on new titles
please contact your bookseller or write to the
publisher.

FOREWORD

The Cortina phenomenon escaped no one's attention in the 1960s. At first glance, there was no reason why the car should have been such a success, for here was a very ordinary-looking car, at once built up to a specification and down to a price. Nonetheless, it tickled the British motorist's fancy like no other family saloon had ever done before. More than a million of the original shape Cortinas were sold in four years, and the restyled car (of 1966-1970) repeated the same trick.

Even so, Ford must have been surprised by the way the 1600E was received. It was introduced in 1967, as a cheap and cheerful way of topping up the image of the Mk II Cortinas, and demand took off like a moon-shot. It was, in fact, the right car at the right time: as sporty-looking as the glamorous Lotus-Cortina with which it shared some parts, as simple as the Cortinas and GTs already being built, but better trimmed and more distinctive than any of them.

Ten years earlier, the 1600E (or a car like it) could never even have been conceived, and had it been the public would never have accepted it, for Fords in the 1950s were still only 'Dagenham Dustbins'. Ten years later, Ford had refined the concept much further, for such a 'sports saloon' is now an inevitable model in every new range.

Many motorists aspired to owning a car like the 1600E in the Swinging Sixties, when it was chic and newsworthy to be trendy, but when it was not necessary to buy real class to cut a dash in the car parks. In the Fifties, to be a Gay Dog ('gay' was an ordinary, acceptable, word too!) you had to buy an MG Magnette, or perhaps a Sunbeam Rapier. Whatever, it had to be very different, and obviously so, from the bread-and-butter saloon of the day. But Ford, and the new, black art of 'Product Planning', changed all that. Using techniques refined in the USA, Ford started to produce wider and ever wider ranges of one basic car, where at least one version was in the 'executive' mould.

Yet the 'executive' trick didn't always work. To be such a strong seller, therefore, the 1600E must have had more than just good looks, wood decoration inside the passenger compartment, and a jazzed-up, sexy, image. It did – it handled like no previous series production Cortina had ever done, and it was the best-equipped Cortina of all. It also had a great deal of character – enough to make it worth the study of a Super Profile, all on its own.

These bare facts – 58,582 Cortina 1600Es built in three years – tell their own story, and everything that follows in the text confirms the reasons for success. When other 'executive' cars of the period have all gone to the last great scrapyard in the sky, there will still be a 1600E cult to keep the cars alive. I hope this slim book explains why.

In writing this volume, I draw on many years of Ford-watching and the mountain of statistics and research material which I have gathered over the years (not forgetting the fact that I owned two Cortina GTs – which were very close relations of the 1600E in all respects – during the 1960s), but I would like to pay special tribute to:

John Danvers, 1600E owner and enthusiast, who might himself have written this book, for supplying some Sections.

Steve Clark and Sheila Knapman of Ford's photographic department, for supplying archive material.

David Burgess-Wise and Martyn Watkins of Ford's public relations division, for supplying many facts and figures.

Don Hilton, of Tricentrol of Dunstable, for guiding me so expertly through the maze of Ford parts and service archives, and for making the very rare Mk II Parts Book available for study.

Thanks also go to *Motor*, *Good Motoring* and *Autosport* for permission to reprint their original roadtests.

And to all 1600E enthusiasts, for keeping the memory of such an interesting car alive.

Graham Robson

HISTORY

It is not possible to relate the story of the 1600E without referring to many other Ford models, so this is not a simple little narrative. Not only was the Cortina 1600E an up-market derivative of the mass-market Mk II Cortina range, but this range had been developed around the same 'chassis' as the original style Cortinas of 1962-1966. Further, Ford were progressively applying the 'E' philosophy to other models at the same time, which adds significance to the whole reason for the 1600E being announced at all. My story, therefore, really begins in 1961.

At that particular time, Ford were building Anglia 105Es (with that strange reverse-slope rear window style), and Mk II Consuls and Zephyrs, while the new Consul Classic (also with reverse-slope rear window styling) was on course for launch in June 1961. All these cars were assembled in the sprawling Dagenham complex, which was beginning to look distinctly over-crowded.

Major expansion, however, was planned, for a brand-new assembly factory was being built at Halewood, on Merseyside, and the building of the Anglias and Classics (and their successors) was to be transferred to that site early in 1963. Dagenham was to be re-equipped completely, and a new mass-market model, later to be

called Cortina, was to be built there.

First thoughts on the Cortina crystallized in 1960, even before the delayed Classic was announced. Ford UK wanted a medium-sized car to be as light, simple and (obviously) as cost-effective to build as possible; the Classic, which had not so much been 'product planned' as 'evolved', was none of those things. Ford of Detroit tentatively offered its British subsidiary the chance to build a front-wheel drive car code-named 'Cardinal', which had been designed in Detroit, but this was a time when the British company still had a great deal of autonomy, and the company's chairman, Sir Patrick Hennessy, turned it down. ('Cardinal' was eventually taken up by Ford of Germany, and put into production as the Taunus 12M and 15M.)

Instead he instructed Fred Hart, as Executive Engineer, Light Car Design, and Terence Beckett, Manager of Product Planning, to evolve a car of entirely British design, using where possible, the engine/transmission/back axle components which had been designed especially for the Anglia, the Classic, and other unspecified developments. The importance of this decision was that it meant that the new car would be using the advanced — and very oversquare — overhead valve engine now known for all time as the 'Kent' series.

Although the thinking, and the talking, began in 1960, after Ford had made an exhaustive study of many current cars including the sensational new BMC Mini, the bare bones of the design were not ready for approval by management until the beginning of 1961. The new project, whimsically code-named 'Archbishop' (as a foil to the USA-designed 'Cardinal', no doubt), was given the go-ahead in January 1961, and all concerned were instructed to have it ready, on sale, and in quantity production, by the motor show of 1962. This left just 21 months to produce a major

new car — a challenging task, even by Ford's demanding standards.

The design, masterminded by Fred Hart, was of a strictly conventional machine, to be offered in two-door saloon, four-door saloon, and five-door estate car forms, with a pressed-steel unit-construction body/chassis, classic front-engine/rear-drive layout, MacPherson strut independent front suspension, and a beam rear axle located and suspended on half-elliptic leaf springs. There were to be two engine sizes — 1.2-litre and 1.5-litre — an all-synchromesh manual gearbox with an automatic transmission option, and a variety of trim levels.

The design/testing/tooling cycle was very tight indeed, which may explain why two very important derivatives — the GT, and the Lotus-Cortina — were not even started until 1962, and were not ready for sale until 1963, though these are the types which, historically, had most to do with the eventual birth of the 1600E.

By dint of furious work by all concerned, the 'Archbishop' project was ready on time, the first pre-production cars being built in May 1962, and the range being announced in September 1962. Since this was a prosperous period when major car manufacturers like Ford could afford frequent model changes, it was planned that the original-shape Cortina would be built for four years, with an important freshening up, or 'face-lift', taking place after two years. In the case of the Mk I Cortina, the face-lift not only involved the introduction of a new grille, but a completely fresh facia style, and the introduction of an advanced new heating and ventilation installation known as 'Aeroflow'.

The Mk I Cortina was an enormous success, not only in the UK, but all round the world, and more than a million were built before the time came to change its shape. In the meantime, too, Ford had embraced the 'Total Performance' philosophy, Walter

Hayes had become the director of public affairs in the UK, and the racing and rallying programmes had taken on ever more fierce and successful aspects. At first with Cortina GTs, and later with Lotus-Cortinas, Ford had stopped being an enthusiastic and cheerful competitor, and became a professional and dedicated winner.

With an eye to announcing a Mk II Cortina in the autumn of 1966, work began on the styling of a new car in 1964, and this is where the first direct historical links with the Cortina 1600E are to be found. The design brief for the new model was simple; new shapes were to be evolved for all derivatives currently offered, which meant that they had to be as suitable for a 1.2-litre 'fleet' model as they would be for the 1.55-litre twin-cam engined Lotus-Cortina.

Even so, there were more limitations this time around, laid down not only by management, but by the growing complexity of the Ford range itself. It is true that the company's small car was still the familiar 105E Anglia, but Ford were planning to introduce a new and rather larger model (coded '1968 Anglia' at this time, but eventually to be named Escort) a year after the new Cortina met its public. In 1963, too, Ford had launched the sharply-styled Corsair, which was effectively a long-wheelbase Cortina under the skin, and before the Mk II Cortina appeared this was due to inherit a new vee-4 engine.

Further, for the Mk II Cortina, the designers were not allowed to design a complete new shell. Instead, they were instructed to use the same pressed-steel floor pan as before, allied to a new superstructure, and to stay within the 14ft overall length established by the original car. The wheelbase, therefore, stayed the same as before, at 8ft 2in, though both front and rear wheel tracks were increased. At the front the increase was 2.5 inches (which helped lower the roll centre, and improve the handling), while at the rear it was 1.5 inches.

The most important mechanical change introduced for the Mk IIs (though it never affected the 1600E) was that the smallest engine became 1297cc, with a five-bearing crankshaft, compared with the 1198cc, three-bearing, engine used in original Cortinas. Further, for the GT and Lotus-Cortina derivatives, there was a new, low-line remote control gear change extension.

At first, when the Mk II Cortina was revealed in October 1966, there was no Lotus-Cortina of any type, nor was the 1600E version even being developed. Mk II 1300s were Type 3014E in Ford's system, and Mk II 1500s were Type 3016E. One reason for the delay in introducing a revised Lotus-Cortina was that there had been a major change of policy regarding this model. Original-shape Lotus-Cortinas had been assembled by Lotus at their factory in Cheshunt, in North London, from body shells supplied by Ford. Product quality, however, had never been the Lotus-Cortina's strong point, and the fact that Lotus were also proposing to move to a new factory at Hethel, near Norwich, persuaded Ford to schedule Mk II Lotus-Cortina assembly 'in house', at Dagenham, on the same line as every other Cortina. In the event, the Type 3020 Lotus-Cortina was not released until March 1967.

At this point, I should also mention a small but important rear suspension change which had been applied to the GT Cortinas from the start of 1965 model year (and 'face-lift') production. To aid the location of the rear axle, twin trailing radius arms had been specified, which pivoted from brackets under the rear seat area. The same system had been adopted for Lotus-Cortinas built from the middle of 1965, was also a feature of the latest Corsair GTs, and was slated for use in the Escort GTs when they were announced in 1968.

Naturally, there were several different levels of trim and equipment, the most luxurious at this time being called 'Super', and even on the GT there was the option of two-door or four-door saloon coachwork. The estate car types were not announced until the beginning of 1967, but these too were offered with various engines (including GT, to special order) and trim levels. The Lotus-Cortina, however, was only ever offered as a two-door saloon.

By this time, Ford were noted for changing their cars fairly regularly, so it was assumed, though never spelled out by Ford, that this MK II Cortina design would be built for about four years, and that there would be one significant face-lift mid-way through this period.

I have not made much of the 1600E at this moment in the Cortina's history, for the simple reason that it had not yet been conceived! In the autumn of 1966, Ford were content to promote their new cars as, 'New Cortina is More Cortina', emphasising that it was more roomy, better equipped, and significantly more luxurious in all respects than the originals.

In the meantime, Ford had also 'invented' the 'executive' car, and were busily planning to extend this philosophy throughout their range. There was nothing new about business executives, but the fact that Rover and Triumph had both introduced 'executive' 2000s in 1963 had caused major upsets in the upper echelons of the fleet-car market. To match this, Ford announced the 2.6-litre Executive Zodiac in January 1965, carried the name over to the vee-6 Mk IV of 1966, and then followed it up by the launch of the Corsair 2000E in January 1967.

The 'E' philosophy was simple and cost-effective, but most successful. To an established model, new styling and furnishing touches were added to make a new type rather more exclusive (E for Executive, E for Exclusive? Nobody cared ...), and this usually meant that there was a wooden facia panel, and new and more plushy seats. Anyone who had studied the Corsair 2000E could surely prophesy what might happen to the Cortina in due course, for there were all the same interior features.

The Corsair 2000E, however, was an important model in the Cortina/Corsair heritage, for it was the first car in which revised, and much more sporting, gear ratios, were fitted. Previous Cortina GTs and Corsair GTs had been inflicted with ratios in which second gear was far too low, and for a time there was a thriving after-market business in supplying different gear sets (to which I personally subscribed with my own GTs). The latest box, dubbed ever afterwards the 'Corsair 2000E' box, was actually for corporate use, and was immediately fitted to Cortina GTs built from the beginning of 1967, and to all MK II Lotus-Cortinas.

Although the Executive Zodiacs had been politely received, and had made their mark, Ford were quite unprepared for the instant success of the Corsair 2000E. By the end of 1967, 40 per cent of all Corsairs being built at Halewood were 2000Es, so readily recognisable on the road by the vinyl roofs, their different styling details, and their special interiors. Even though a 2000E cost £1008 at a time when the ordinary Corsair 2000 sold for £879, the customers still saw it as a bargain. Ford's managers, for their part, saw it as a miracle, because the 2000E was much the more profitable of the two cars for them actually to build!

It was the dramatic boom in the Corsair 2000E's popularity which then spurred Ford's product planners to develop a similar 'executive' Cortina, and it was only as late as this – the spring of 1967 – that the 1600E, coded 3036E inside the design departments, began to take shape. Not only was there an obvious demand for this

type of car, but there was also a ready-made gap to be filled in the Cortina range: at the beginning of 1967, the four-door GT cost £865, and the newly-announced Lotus-Cortina £1068.

As one Ford manager has since confirmed, 'We created the 1600E to fill a gap. We wanted a four-door model that would fit between the GT and the Lotus, offering sporty performance without complications. So the twin-cam engine was out, because of the possible warranty costs.' (He did not say, but might also have done so, that a four-door twin-cam engine model would have had to be priced even higher than that asked for the Lotus-Cortina).

The very first 3036E 'prototype' was actually a car mocked up with Cortina GT mechanicals, and Lotus-Cortina suspension and wheels. Senior product planners I talked to confirmed that it did not look right until the distinctive Rostyle wheels were added to the specification. In effect, the car needed no long-term open-road development, as all its mechanical components were already well proven in one Cortina or another. Once the level of equipment, and the decorative package, had been settled, all that remained was for it to be released for production in that form.

It is tempting to describe the new car as a four-door GT with Lotus-Cortina suspension, and a party frock and make-up, but the 1600E, as it was soon christened, was really much more carefully developed than this. As a sweeping statement, the description will do, but in detail it falls well short.

The basic decision Ford took at first was that the new car should be an 'E', one of their successful new 'executive' cars, and that they would call it by its engine size, to make it stand in line with, and slightly below, the 2000E. It was also decided that it should only be built in four-door saloon form – no two-door type like the Lotus-Cortina being considered at first,

presumably because it was thought that 'executive' car occupants would not want to struggle past the front seats to gain access to the rear.

The basis of the design, to be introduced in October 1967, was to be that of the 1968 model-year Cortina GT. The 1968 designation, as opposed to the 1967 designation, is very important in this context, for it was the point at which Ford phased in a series of very important mid-term improvements, not only to the engines of all Cortinas, but to the transmission, the suspension, and the equipment in general.

The truly major change was to the engines. At this point, the 'Kent' four-cylinder engines, which had already been in production in one form or another since the summer of 1959, were treated to a major redesign. All types had entirely new cross-flow cylinder heads, where the combustion space was largely contained in the crown of the pistons, while the larger of the two engines was pushed up from 1499cc to 1599cc; this was achieved by using a longer stroke, and the block casting was made slightly deeper to make this possible. It meant that the peak output figures for the GT engine went up from 78 bhp at 5200 rpm/91 lbf ft at 3600 rpm, to 88 bhp at 5400 rpm/96 lbf ft at 3600 rpm. Although the peak torque figure was little higher than before, the bigger engine was much more flexible, and pulled more strongly from low engine speeds.

Because of these changes, which were applied to all 'Kent' engines, the carburettors found themselves on the right-hand side of the engine bay instead of the left, though the exhaust manifold and pipe run stayed on the left as before. At the same time, other improvements made to the Cortina GT included the standardisation of radial-ply tyres, and the fitment of a clock to the centre console.

The new 1600E, which was not revealed at the same time as

7

the 1968-model Cortinas (they were launched in mid-September 1967, whereas the 1600E made its public bow at the Paris show at the beginning of October), was finalised on the basis of this uprated Cortina GT package, and was almost, but not quite, a 100 mph car in standard form.

Under the four-door saloon body shell, the 'chassis' was a mixture of Cortina GT and Lotus-Cortina, with special differences into the bargain. The engine, transmission, and back axle, were pure 1600GT in all respects (the legend '1600GT' appeared on the rocker cover, in any case), which is to say that the uprated '2000E' gearbox ratios were employed, and that there was the neat remote control gear change, now with the circular clock mounted ahead of it on the console. Ford did not offer the option of automatic transmission on Cortina GTs or Lotus-Cortinas, and did not propose to do so on the 1600E either; they never changed that policy.

The simple way to describe the 1600E's stance is to say that it was lower than the Cortina GT, because it used the shorter front struts, lowered rear leaf spring suspension and stiffer spring/damper settings of the Mk II Lotus-Cortina – except that it was *not* as simple as that. The official Ford parts book lists several different sets of springs and dampers in the time that the 1600E was in production – some of which were Lotus-Cortina, and some of which were not! Most cars, however, seem to have used Lotus settings, which made the car more squat, with better handling, than the GT from which it was derived.

At the rear of the car the axle was located by twin trailing radius arms, while the new and fashionable pressed-steel Rostyle road wheels, with 5.5in rims, and 165-section India Autoband radial-ply tyres, were standardised. The complication, as far as the radius arms are concerned, is that they were dropped from Home-Market

and *some* Export Cortina GTs from the beginning of 1968, to improve the cars' refinement, but they were always retained on 1600Es, where presumably a refinement improvement would have been welcome!

The 1600E, of course, was distinguishable by a great deal of extra equipment. On the outside of the car, apart from the presence of the special wheels, and the near-to-the-ground stance, a 1600E could always be recognised by the use of a black (Lotus-Cortina type) grille, extra Wipac driving lamps, automatic reversing lamps, and the '1600E' badging under the Cortina script on the boot lid. Many cars were fitted with rubber faced over-riders, which were a Ford accessory. A pair of distinctive, but completely anonymous, emblems were mounted – one on each rear quarter panel behind the doors, but, unlike the Corsair 2000E, the Cortina 1600E was never fitted with a vinyl roof as standard.

Inside the car, although the general mechanical equipment was that of the Cortina GT, there were quite remarkable upgradings all round the car. The layout of the instruments and controls was exactly like that of the Cortina GT, which is to say that there were matching speedometer and rev-counter dials ahead of the driver's eyes but tucked away behind the new steering wheel (which had light alloy spokes perforated with circular 'lightening' holes, and a padded, imitation-leather, rim), while there were four auxiliary instruments (ammeter, oil pressure, water temperature and fuel contents) in a line, high up under a hump in the crash roll which covered the top of the facia. The radio was standard, and there was a clock in the centre console ahead of the gear lever, which was itself treated to a gaiter. The instrument panel and the glove box lid, were covered by slabs of thick, highly polished wood, whose grain was matched on the cappings along the top rails of all four doors.

Reclining front seats were standard, and all were as plushy as any so far fitted to a Ford Cortina. The centre console oddments box of the Cortina GT and Lotus-Cortina was retained, static front seat belts were fitted, and the handbrake lever was of the pull-out type, mounted in a ratchet to the left-hand (centre of the car) side of the steering column.

The heating and ventilation system was up to the usual high Ford standards, and there was even a partially carpeted boot floor, and a cover for the spare wheel. Cortinas had certainly changed!

The 1600E, of course, would never have been a success had the road behaviour not been right, and had the price been too high. As to the price, no one was complaining, for Ford set the level exactly right. In October 1967, when the new car went on sale, the price of a 1600GT, with all taxes paid, was £890, and that of a Lotus-Cortina was £1080, while that of the 1600E – no less sporting than the GT, and better trimmed than any other Cortina – was priced at £982, almost exactly in the middle of that gap.

The initial reaction of testers to the car's behaviour and its equipment, too, was encouraging, particularly as the 1600E seemed to have lost none of the sporting characteristics of the GT or the Lotus-Cortina in favour of a more plushy specification. John Bolster, writing in *Autosport* in March 1968, was quite ecstatic about the roadholding, for instance:

'The roadholding, assisted by radial-ply tyres, is superb – no lesser word suffices. On wet roads or dry, the driver gains complete confidence, and the handling is absolutely predictable. The steering is quick and precise, feeling so right all the time, and the wheels seem glued to the road, irrespective of surface ...'

All of which was true, as far as it went, but no one could hide the fact that the 1600E had a very firm ride, which was quite unavoidable due to the Lotus-Cortina (or nearly so, as explained above) settings. *Autocar's* testers liked the handling and the steering when they tried a car in December 1967, but they also reported that ride was notably harsher than might be expected from a car of that class. Although I am tempted to say that *Autocar* was entirely missing the very point of the 1600E (it was a surrogate Lotus-Cortina to many people), I must agree that the hard ride was the least satisfactory aspect of the car.

No one, of course, was disappointed with the level of equipment, and the general level of performance was considered acceptable; a top speed of 98 mph, 0-60mph acceleration in under 12 seconds, and overall fuel consumption of around 25 mpg.

Overall, the 1600E offered brisk motoring in a very attractive package, and Ford dealers looked forward to a healthy demand for the cars when the winter of 1967-68 was over. However, neither they, nor their acquaintances at Ford, could have visualised what would happen next.

EVOLUTION

The best way to summarize the life and times of the 1600E is merely to say: 'Look at the figures'. I am sure I am not exaggerating at all when I suggest that the career of the 1600E was an amazing, and quite unexpected success story for Ford. The bare facts are that in less than three full years, more cars were sold and – this was important – more hearts were won over, than could ever have been forecast in advance. Although it took a few months for the word to be passed round and for the car's reputation to become known, once cars started to be delivered, and orders to flow in, the 1600E became something of a self-generating phenomenon.

Demand did not peak early, then quietly fade away as the trendies began to look elsewhere for their fashionable thrills – for more 1600Es were sold in 1969 than in 1968, and even more in 1970. The rate went up and up, with the two highest production months of all at Dagenham coming in June and July 1970, just before the entire Cortina Mk II range was dropped in favour of the very transatlantic Mk IIIs which replaced them.

David Burgess-Wise, Ford's resident historian, has generously supplied me with a complete table

of production statistics, for 1600Es actually assembled at Dagenham, and this tells a fascinating story. After a gentle start, with just 2524 1600Es being built in 1967, there were 11,385 in 1968, 17,807 in 1969, and 17,501 in part of 1970. But there is even more to the 1600E's success story than this, for thousands of cars were supplied to other Ford factories, notably to Amsterdam in Holland, in kit form, to swell the totals. All in all, 58,582 1600Es were eventually built, which must have made Ford's managers, and accountants, very happy indeed. The vital statistics are given in a table at the end of this Section.

The table shows that the first series-production 1600Es were built in September 1967, and that more than 40 cars a day were being built in October, when the car made its show debuts in Paris, and at Earls Court. First exports came in November, but these were at a relatively low rate until the Spring of 1969. From Dagenham, however, the 1600E was essentially a home-market car, as the figures prove.

Virtually no cars were built in May 1968, which indicates that there was a shortage of some essential 1600E component, for the charts I have seen show that all other Cortinas continued to be built at their usual rate. There was also a two-month hiatus in October/November/December 1968, before full production of the modified 1969-model cars could get started, and when Ford's resources were concentrated on the 'bread-and-butter' Cortinas.

After that, it was merely a case of building as many 1600Es as the planners could find space for at Dagenham. The last few cars were built in August 1970, immediately before the annual holiday shut-down, after which the facilities at Dagenham were completely turned over to building Cortina Mk IIIs. No successor to the 1600E was then produced.

The 1969-model 'face lift'

The most significant evolutionary changes to the 1600E were made after only one year, when the entire Cortina Mk II range was revised, and freshened up, at mid-term in its four-year run. Some changes were applied across the board, the 1600E benefiting accordingly, and some changes were specifically made for the higher-performance models. It is worth noting, too, that the Escort Twin-Cam had been put on sale by this time, which took some of the limelight away from the 'hot' Cortinas, even though they continued to sell as well as ever.

The most important mechanical improvement for the 1969 models was that a new type of gearbox casing, and remote control change mechanism were introduced. Early Mk II GTs and 1600Es had used a three-selector rail gearbox with a 'low-line' remote extension, but for 1969 there was a new single-rail selector mechanism, and a different remote control layout. On the original box, the reverse gear slot in the gate had been towards the right, and back, but for the single rail box it was towards the left, and forward.

At the same time, the centre console of these cars was redesigned, the central cubby box was deleted, and a pull-up handbrake was located between the seats, rather than a pull-out lever being under the facia. Ordinary Cortinas which did not have a console had always had the between-seats handbrake, in any case.

Also inside the car, the facia style of GT/1600E/Lotus-Cortina models was revised. The line of four auxiliary instruments was lowered by several inches (so that no crash-roll binnacle was needed any longer), heating and ventilation controls were relocated to make way for this change, and certain switches were repositioned. There was a new wooden facia board for the 1600E, obviously, and the front end of the centre console was restyled, and swept up to meet the facia, with the clock rather higher than before, and with the push-button radio styled into the top of that console.

A new type of rear seating was provided, effectively with twin 'bucket' seats, Rover 2000 style, and a fold-down arm rest, while all seats were treated to a perforated type of synthetic material. External style changes included the use of a matt-black panel across the tail between the tail lamps, with chrome strips above and below it, and the addition of FORD letters across the nose of the bonnet and the lip of the boot lid.

An internal bonnet release was specified, while there was also a fully-fused electrical system. At the same time, the finish of the Rostyle wheels was changed, to save on cost. Instead of the chrome plating on the 'spokes', these were treated to aluminium paint instead.

The rare two-door 1600E

Here in the UK, we missed the announcement of a two-door 1600E, for 1969, for the simple reason that it was never sold on this market, but was definitely 'For Export Only'; officially, no two-door 1600Es were ever delivered to British customers. Actual production of two-door models began at Dagenham in January 1969, and continued steadily until July 1970, though it never reached the rate achieved by four-door models. In 19 months, only 1083

two-doors were built at Dagenham, of a total of 2749 in all, which includes kits.

Mechanically, all the two-door 1600Es were like the four-door cars, except they had left-hand drive. There were, however, minor but important differences in trim and decoration. The two-door shells, of course, were those used by other two-door Cortinas, including GTs and Lotus-Cortinas, and this meant that the appropriate fold-forward front seats had to be used. Where appropriate (and where made necessary by local legal requirements) the new Ford 'safety' steering wheel, instead of the smart polished light-alloy 1600E wheel, had to be used, and at the rear of the car there was normally no matt-black painted band between the tail lamp clusters, nor the smart, thin, coach line along the car's flank, from nose to tail.

The End, and the Aftermath

The end came for the 1600E in August 1970, when it was still not yet over the peak of its popularity;

at the same time, too, the last of the Lotus-Cortinas was built. Neither was replaced, for the new Cortina Mk III range included GTs and GXLs, complete with the new 2.0-litre Pinto engines, but no 'E' and 'Lotus' derivatives. It was not for some time that Ford realised that they had abandoned a phenomenon, with demand still unsatisfied, and when they came to launch a Mk III called 2000E it was too late. There was no truly sporting GT or Lotus from which to derive a 2000E; the Mk III did not look as good as the old car had done, and certainly did not handle as well.

From that moment on, the 1600E was an appreciating 'classic', and now has a permanent home in the mythology of sporting 'old' Fords,

1600E Production at Dagenham – September 1967 to August 1970

This is the way in which 1600E assembly progressed at Dagenham, month by month, in the three years that it was in production. There was a clean start and a clean finish to its short career, for 1600Es were phased in as the first 'cross-flow' Cortinas were assembled for the 1968 model year, and phased out with all other Mk II Cortinas, to make way for the entirely different Mk IIIs launched in the autumn of 1970

Month		Home	Export		Total	
1600E 4-door saloon (2-door saloon in brackets)						
1967	September	56	–		56	
	October	834	–		834	
	November	609	41		650	
	December	932	52		984	
1968	January	1198	137		1335	
	February	1080	121		1201	
	March	1085	97		1182	
	April	959	82		1041	
	May	13	2		15	
	June	204	49		253	
	July	1395	480		1875	
	August (Holiday month)	956	140		1096	
	September	773	51		824	
	October (1968 model)	1277	11		1228	
	October (1969 model)	3	–		3	
	November	2	–		2	
	December	286	–		286	
1969	January	695	100	(128)	795	(128)
	February	1440	918	(69)	2358	(69)
	March	790	184	(13)	974	(13)
	April	1283	348	(30)	1631	(30)
	May	1257	354	(85)	1611	(85)
	June	550	249	(45)	799	(45)
	July	1268	255	(41)	1523	(41)
	August (Holiday month)	670	152	(45)	822	(45)
	September	1553	241	(76)	1794	(76)
	October	625	267	(78)	892	(78)
	November	1919	479	(34)	2398	(34)
	December	1284	211	(71)	1495	(71)
1970	January	2066	253	(37)	2319	(37)
	February	1632	216	(82)	1848	(82)
	March	2196	423	(92)	2619	(92)
	April	1983	272	(46)	2255	(46)
	May	1908	211	(34)	2119	(34)
	June	2662	359	(33)	3021	(33)
	July	2592	327	(44)	2919	(44)
	August	29	4	(–)	33	(–)

2-door 1600Es were never officially built for the Home Market. These production figures do not tie up with complete 1600E totals of 55,833 four-door saloon and 2749 two-door saloon types, as cars were sent to other Ford plants (notably Cork, in the Republic of Ireland) as CKD kits, for local assembly.

SPECIFICATION

Type designation	Ford Cortina 1600E. (Type 3036E in Ford system).
Built	Dagenham, England. September 1967 – August 1970.
Numbers made	55,833 four-door, 2,749 two-door. (All two-door cars for export markets)
Drive configuration	Front engine, rear-wheel-drive. Transmission in unit with engine. Open propeller shaft to 'live' rear axle.
Engine Type	Updated 'crossflow' Ford 'Kent' design. Cast iron block and opposed manifold cylinder head, bowl-in-piston combustion chambers, four-cylinders in-line, pushrod-operated overhead valves, camshaft in side of block.
Capacity	1598.8 cc (97.6 cu in).
Compression ratio	9.2 : 1
Bore and stroke	80.97 x 77.62 mm (3.19 x 3.06 in)
Maximum power	88 bhp at 5400 rpm (net).
Maximum torque	96 lb ft (13.3 kg m) at 3600 rpm (net).
Carburettor	Weber 32 DFM compound dual choke downdraught, differential throttle opening.
Transmission	Four speed, all-synchromesh gearbox, mounted in-line with engine and driven through 7.54 in (19.2 cm) hydraulically operated, self adjusting, single plate diaphragm clutch. Internal gearbox ratios: 2.97, 2.01, 1.40, 1.00, reverse 3.32:1. Overall ratios: 1st – 11.591, 2nd – 7,839, 3rd – 5.448, 4th – 3.900, Reverse – 12.964 : 1.
Final drive	Hypoid, semi-floating rear axle. Ratio: 3.90 : 1, (Optional 4.125 : 1).
Structure	Welded-up sheet steel monocoque body/chassis unit.
Wheelbase	98 in (248.9 cm)
Track	Front: 52.5 in (133 cm), Rear: 51.0 in (129 cm).

Suspension	Front:	Independent, coil springs, Macpherson struts incorporating telescopic double action shock absorbers, with anti-roll bar and track control arms.
	Rear:	Half-elliptic leaf springs (five leaves per spring), hydraulic double action telescopic shock absorbers, axle location assisted by twin radius arms.

Steering

Burman recirculating ball. Ratio: 15.7 : 1.
Leather covered, aluminium three-spoke steering wheel 15.25 in dia.
4.25 turns lock-to-lock.
Turning circle 30 ft (9.15 m).

Brakes	Front:	Girling, hydraulically operated disc brakes, 9.62in (24.4cm) dia. forward facing calipers.
	Rear:	Girling, hydraulically operated self-adjusting drum brakes 9in (22.9cm) dia. (Optional vacuum servo assistance and dual line system).

Wheels and tyres

Pressed steel 'Rostyle' flat ledge rims and 5.5in rim width.
165 x 13 India Autoband radial-ply tubeless tyres on most new cars.

Bodywork

Steel, integral construction, safety glass all round. All doors fitted with zero torque anti-burst locks. Air extraction vents on rear quarter pillars. Separate luggage compartment, capacity 21.0 cu ft (0.592 cu m) gross. Covered spare wheel housed in nearside of luggage compartment.

Dimensions

Overall length 168.0in (426.7cm).
Overall width 64.9in (164.8cm).
Overall height (normal laden) (54.7in (138.9cm).
Ground clearance (normal laden) minimum 5.15in (13.1cm).

Weight

1,992lbs (906kg).

Electrical system		12 volt negative earth.
	Charging:	Lucas C40L dynamo (25 amp), Lucas 37342 or Autolite GR5001 regulator, 57 amp hr battery. (Some early models fitted with Lucas C40 dynamo (22 amp), Lucas 37344 or Autolite GR5000 regulator, 38 amp hr battery).
	Ignition:	12 volt coil (oil filled) and distributor. Automatic control by governor weights and manifold vacuum.
	Lighting:	Lucas sealed filament, 60/45 watts. Wipac driving lamps, 48 watts (wired through main beam).

Performance

Maximum speed (mean) 98 m.p.h.
Speed in gears:
    3rd gear 73 mph
    2nd gear 51 mph
    1st gear 35 mph
Acceleration, 0 – 60 mph: 13.1 sec.
Standing start $\frac{1}{4}$ mile: 18.8 sec.
Acceleration in gears:
    Top: 20 – 40 mph, 11.5 sec.
    50 – 70 mph, 12.1 sec.
    Third: 20 – 40 mph, 6.4 sec,
    50 – 70 mph, 8.1 sec.
    Second: 20 – 40 mph, 4.8 sec.
Fuel consumption: 25.1 mpg overall.

ROAD TESTS

FORD CORTINA 1600E

THE Ford Cortina is a very successful car. Probably even its makers never expected that it would become such a favourite, especially as it followed the Classic, which sunk without trace. Right from the start, the car appealed because it was the ideal size and it combined a lively performance with good roadholding. When the time came for restyling, Fords endowed the once homely Cortina with continental *chic,* which further increased its appeal.

To match the new appearance, the performance has now been increased by the adoption of a crossflow engine. In the case of the 1300, this has a pure Heron head with a flat surface, the combustion chambers being recessed into the piston tops. The previous 1500 cc engine has been replaced by a 1600 cc unit, which has now become a more popular size, and in this case the bore remains the same at 80.98 mm, but there is a taller cylinder block to accommodate the extra stroke of 77.62 mm. A bowl-in-piston combustion chamber is again used, but the head is not completely flat, having shallow combustion chambers in which the valves seat, permitting the deletion of the "spectacles" for valve head clearance which are machined in the piston tops of the 1300.

The cylinder head, in both versions, now has the inlet and exhaust manifolds on opposite sides. A considerable increase in power output is given, but it is the improved torque for acceleration in the middle ranges

Ford's smallest executive saloon packs plenty of punch

which is the main feature, most valuable for quick overtaking without exceeding the speed limit.

The larger engine benefits from the new design and it also gains more torque from its extra 100 cc compared with its predecessor. The GT version, which is the subject of the present test, has a special camshaft and a Weber twin-choke downdraught carburetter of the compound type. This gives it an extra 10 bhp (net) over last year's model but the greater efficiency of the design is also reflected in better fuel consumption figures at all speeds.

Perhaps the most important mechanical improvement is the restaging of the gearbox ratios. The previous GT model was cursed with an extremely low second gear, and this has been rectified, both first and second speeds now having considerably higher maxima. This not only improves the performance but makes smooth driving

much easier, now that the wide gap between third and second gears has been reduced. The well-tried chassis design is naturally retained, with MacPherson strut and lower wishbone front suspension and semi-elliptics behind, plus trailing links. The suspension is lowered as in the Lotus Cortina.

The car chosen for our test was the 1600E. Fords have already entered the executive market with their V6 Zodiac and they have now very wisely given the treatment to a model which is of more convenient size for many people in England. There is a considerable demand for a car which has the luxury of a craftsman-built limousine allied with the many practical advantages of a popular mass-production chassis.

The 1600E can at once be distinguished by its highly decorative wheels. This type of wheel may look rather absurd on some cars, but it seems to suit the lines of

AUTOSPORT, MARCH 29, 1968

the Ford and certainly makes it look different. Inside, there is lots of polished wood everywhere which some people might consider old-fashioned, but it attracted much admiration, both from passengers and casual passers-by. The driver has a splendid display of proper round instruments and a leather-covered steering wheel to make him feel good. Naturally, the power unit is the GT version of the new 1600.

On the road, the 1600E is noticeably much livelier than previous Cortinas. These cars have sometimes been criticized for lacking "punch" in the middle ranges, but nobody can ever say that again, and it is difficult to believe that the engine has a capacity of less than 2 litres. The car is certainly ideal for this country with its 70 mph limit, and third gear, which will just exceed this speed, gives really vivid acceleration to regain the legal cruising speed. The new higher second gear is an absolute delight—one could hardly imagine that a single alteration would do so much for a car—and it is no longer necessary to remain in third gear round sharp corners.

The car will cruise with great ease at 70 to 80 mph, which is its best speed. From 85 mph upwards, the engine is obviously doing more work and it is considerably noisier, but it will eventually attain about 95 mph, which is indicated as well over 100 mph on the speedometer. Incidentally, an executive would surely need a trip reading on his speedometer for timing his individual journeys. Driven hard, the 1600E records not less than 25 mpg in open country.

In town, the performance is not quite so outstanding. This is partly due to the clutch, which does not match the excellence of the gearbox, tending to be heavy in action with rather a long travel on the pedal. The engine is not very flexible at low speeds, and it seems best to forget about top gear in London. Above 30 mph, the car suddenly comes alive, and it retains a useful performance even when one is too lazy to use the gearlever. Certainly, most owners will prefer to employ the gearbox to the full, for the remote control gearlever is a joy to handle.

The roadholding, assisted by radial ply tyres, is superb—no lesser word suffices. On wet roads or dry, the driver gains complete confidence, and the handling is absolutely predictable. The steering is quick and precise, feeling so right all the time, and the wheels seem glued to the road, irrespective of surface. The ride is not soft, and there is some up and down movement on certain country roads, but under more normal conditions the driver and his passengers travel in comfort. The brakes are progressive and stand up well to quite hard driving without smelling excessively hot.

The Ford heating and ventilation system has often been praised. It is certainly excellent, and this is one of the few cars which can be warm inside without being stuffy. It actually seems possible to control the heat, without the "all or nothing" effect which most heaters give. It also adds to the pleasure of riding in the car to be seated in such a well-furnished interior.

It was Laurence Pomeroy the elder, I think, who said that if you have to use a stopwatch to find out whether you have made an improvement or not, you have not made a worthwhile improvement. In their crossflow engine, Fords have an improvement that needs no stopwatch for proof. Particularly under present day road conditions, the Cortina, in all its versions, is now a far better car. When this new performance is allied with superior comfort and appearance, the Cortina becomes a most desirable possession and I predict an enthusiastic demand for the 1600E, the Cortina for the VIP.

AUTOSPORT, MARCH 29, 1968

SPECIFICATION AND PERFORMANCE DATA

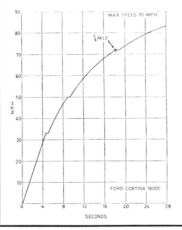

Car tested: Ford Cortina 1600E 4-door saloon, price £1020 18s 11d including PT.

Engine: Four-cylinders, 80.98 mm x 77.62 mm (1599 cc). Pushrod operated overhead valves. Compression ratio 9.2:1. 93 (gross) bhp at 5400 rpm. Weber twin-choke downdraught carburetter. Lucas coil and distributor.

Transmission: Single dry plate clutch. 4-speed all-synchromesh gearbox with central remote control, ratios 1.0, 1.40, 2.01, and 2.97:1. Open propeller shaft. Hypoid rear axle, ratio 3.90:1.

Chassis: Combined pressed-steel body and chassis. Independent front suspension by MacPherson struts with lower wishbones and anti-roll bar. Burman recirculating ball steering gear. Live rear axle on semi-elliptic springs and trailing links. Telescopic dampers all round. Bolt-on pressed steel wheels with chromium decoration, fitted 165 x 13 radial ply tyres. Girling disc front and drum rear brakes.

Equipment: 12-volt lighting and starting. Speedometer. Rev counter. Ammeter. Oil pressure, water temperature, and fuel gauges. Clock. Heating, demisting and ventilation system. Windscreen wipers and washers. Flashing direction indicators. Cigar lighter. Paired driving lamps. Reversing light. Radio (extra).

Dimensions: Wheelbase, 8 ft 2 ins; track (front), 4 ft 4.5 ins; (rear), 4 ft 3 ins; overall length, 14 ft; width, 5 ft 4.9 ins; weight, 18 cwt 16 lbs.

Performance: Maximum speed, 95 mph. Speeds in gears: third, 72 mph; second, 50 mph; first, 33 mph. Standing quarter-mile, 18.3 s. Acceleration: 0-30 mph, 4.2 s; 0-50 mph, 9 s; 0-60 mph, 12.4 s; 0-80 mph, 25 s.

Fuel consumption: 24 to 28 mpg.

GM ROAD TEST -1

Ford Cortina 1600E

JERRY AMES

SHORTLY before the last Paris Show, Ford unveiled yet another Cortina—the 1600E. This time, the new model is specially created to appeal to young, " with it " executives, determined to go places—usually in a hurry.

So the 1600E is fast, distinctive in appearance and has those extra touches of refinement that sets it in a class apart from ordinary family saloons.

The 1600E is a development of the GT Cortina, the E standing for Executive. Ford, with their vast experience of catering for the needs of business motorists, have produced a unique, modestly priced vehicle that is right on target for the up and coming generation. It may not have the smooth opulence of a director's car costing more than twice as much, but at least it is a step in this direction.

Restyled Wheels

Based on the GT Cortina, the 1600E has the lower, firmer suspension of the Cortina Lotus and with wide, 5½in wheels, smartly restyled with thicker spokes that give the appearance of magnesium alloy, a matt black front grille containing two headlamps and a

Built with the young in mind, the 1600E has startling saloon performance

pair of main beam spots, it is a very different looking car from the GT.

The 1600E engine with Weber compound carburetter develops 88 bhp net at 5400 rpm and with kerb weight of 18cwt has an extremely useful power to weight ratio, which is reflected by the very lively performance.

The front engine transmits its power to the rear wheels through a 7½in diaphragm clutch and a splendid 4-speed all synchromesh gearbox. Suspension is independent at the front only, while sizeable disc/drum brakes cope adequately with high speeds.

This is a car in which it is desirable to make good use of the 4-speed box if full performance is sought, although this should pose no hardship to energetic young executives.

The floor gear lever is conveniently positioned in a central console. Changes up or down can be precise and very quick, for it is almost impossible to beat the powerful synchromesh. Although the box does not have close ratios, they are satisfactorily spaced for its purpose and the lower gears allow maxima of 74, 52 and 34 mph.

For a nicely finished saloon with a capacity of only 1600 cc, the E is a very fast car. When pushed hard it can return a maximum of 97 mph, so cruising speeds of 80-85 mph are well within its scope.

At high speeds the engine is inclined to feel harsh, a not uncommon feature of some highly tuned units, although this is not likely to be of any great concern to younger executives, who will be so full of praise for its rapid performance; older drivers might be a little more critical.

The engine starts easily on full choke and fairly soon reaches a satis-

A wooden facia sets off a fine array of instruments, with a clock below

factory working temperature; but most of its power is at the top end, so at speeds of 25 mph in top gear it indicates a need to engage a lower gear to avoid uneven, snatchy running.

But the 1600E can beat most others away from the traffic lights and this is a point that will weigh strongly in its favour with the younger set. When making a hurried standing start, the 1600E can reach 50 mph in 8½ seconds and be up to 70 mph in just over 16 seconds. There are extremely few saloons that can get near these figures. The use of radius arms at the rear has almost eliminated wheel hop when accelerating hard and they are a useful contribution to quicker getaway.

With the broader wheels, a suspension that is lower than the standard GT and the new India Autoband tyres, wheelgrip and cornering are far above average, even for a quick saloon. This is a young man's car; it is drivers in the lower age group who will be more ready to exploit the full possibilities of its exceptional road holding and handling.

Excellent Road Holding

Wet or dry surfaces seem to make little difference to its leech-like road grip, a comforting thought to those expected to travel far and fast in a day's motoring.

The recirculating ball steering is not quite so low geared as some modern cars, needing just under four turns from lock to lock. It has a slightly dead feel, but is not too heavy at slow and parking speeds.

Today, fuel consumption with all cars should be considered in relation to performance and not merely judged by engine capacity. In this respect the 1600E shows up well; when pushed hard it will be no better than 23 mpg, but driven more leisurely it can improve to around 27 mpg.

The Girling disc drum brakes, using equipment of adequate size, provide very satisfactory stopping from moderate pedal pressures. Constant hard use from speeds around 60 mph shows they are free from fade. The handbrake holds with ease on gradients of 1 in 5½, but when used as an emergency brake to slow the car, it can quite easily lock a wheel.

This is a common fault with the handbrakes of almost every make of car in the present age. In my opinion, it is the wrong idea, one of the bad design features imported from America with which we are still stuck. Handbrakes should revert to their original purpose and become usable, emergency brakes

TEST DATA—FORD CORTINA 1600E			
PERFORMANCE		**SPEEDS**	
0–30 mph	3.9 sec	Top:	97 mph
0–40	5.8	Third:	74
0–50	8.5	Second:	52
0–60	11.7	Bottom:	34
0–70	16.3	Fuel consumption: 23–27 mpg	
0–80	23.4	Fuel capacity: 10 gall.	

ENGINE: 4-cylinder ohv push rod. Bore and stroke 81 mm × 77.6 mm, capacity 1599 cc. Compression ratio 9 to 1. Develops 88 bhp at 5400 rpm. Max. torque 96lb ft at 3600 rpm. Carburetter, Weber 32 DFM compound.
TRANSMISSION: Clutch 7.5in Borg and Beck. Four speed all synchromesh gearbox. Ratios: top direct; third 1.40; second 2.01; bottom 2.97. Hypoid bevel final drive 3.91.
DETAILS: Suspension independent front only by MacPherson strut, enclosing coil spring, lower wishbone and roll bar. Rear: live axle, leaf springs and upper radius arms. Telescopic dampers. Brakes: Girling 9⅜in front discs, 9in rear drums. Tyres: India Autoband 165 × 13. Steering: Burman recirculating ball.
DIMENSIONS: Wheelbase 8ft 2in. Track (f) 4ft 5¾in, (r) 4ft 4½in. Overall length 14ft; width 5ft 5½in; height 4ft 8in. Turning circle 28ft. Weight 18cwt.
PRICE (inc. delivery charge but not safety belts): Basic £799. With P.T. £1,021.

as well as for parking. A little more development work is needed on them.

All four doors give easy access to front and rear seats of the 1600E. Those in the front have backs adjustable for rake and can provide reasonable room for the long-legged. There is still ample knee and foot room for rear seat passengers.

The driver faces a bold array of easy to read instruments set in a wooden facia that makes a pleasant change from modern, cold-looking plastic. The smallish, 3-spoke steering wheel is leather covered; centrally mounted heat controls are simple to operate and there are directional air

vents on either side of the facia, while direction indicators, headlamp flashing and dipping are operated by a single stalk switch. A clock is provided on the console forward of the gearbox.

The interior layout and equipment of the 1600E is well up to executive standard, while a large rear boot can easily swallow a good deal of luggage. Servicing is called for at 6,000 mile intervals, the essential items being conveniently accessible.

Essentially a younger man's saloon, Ford's Cortina 1600E has most of the desirable features that should appeal to an ambitious young executive. Not the least being its thrusting performance.

The engine has a Weber compound carburetter and develops 88 bhp at 5400 rpm

MOTOR ROAD TEST No.8/68 ● Ford Cortina 1600E

Enjoyable extrovert

Luxury Cortina; good performance and roadholding; indifferent ride; too much noise; extras good value

AMERICAN manufacturers can easily produce 10,000 variations on a basic model without a repeat, so it is hardly surprising that those car makers in Britain that get nearest to this model proliferation have American parentage. It is perhaps the success of the bolt-on goodie trade that has inspired Ford, Rootes and Vauxhall to take the plunge into the option game on their basic themes. With a little more power and/or a little more trim a manufacturer can manipulate his model into a completely different market.

Ford started on the power theme, enlarging the original Cortina 1200 to 1500, GT and then Lotus tunes, repeating themselves in the new shape. But it was not really until the appearance of the Corsair 2000E that they tapped the market which requires more obvious evidence of the best car in the range. To the Cortina GT—a brisk five-seater saloon—Ford have added extras which two different types of clientele could only add for themselves at greater cost from outside sources. E really stands for Executive—as in the Zodiac but on a lesser scale; to appeal to these "junior" executives the 1600E boasts a woodlined interior and a facia more reminiscent of a Jaguar's, a gold line down the side, reclining seats, fancy wheels and the new, squatter look which

suggests that the owner might be as get-ahead as the car undoubtedly is on performance.

On its other front, where E might stand for Enthusiast (or even Extrovert), the new squat look serves a more useful purpose than just appearance; it follows from having the Cortina Lotus suspension—firmer and lower—and 5½J steel wheels cleverly styled to look like mag alloy ones. The handling and roadholding are now extremely good, particularly so on wet and greasy roads, where the India Autobands seem to excel. In fact, from a keen driver's view point there is little to complain of in the 1600E; with the standard GT engine it goes well—maximum of 96.3 m.p.h. and 0–60 m.p.h. in 11.8s.—and has only a moderate thirst for petrol, our overall consumption of 23.1 m.p.g. being pretty fair for a hard driven 18½ cwt., five-seater saloon.

It is on the Executive front that the car is not quite up to its label. It looks attractively aggressive (or vice versa) and the interior is well styled and finished but it is not particularly restful on the open road. The ride is jerky, there is too much wind noise at all out-of-town speeds, and engine harshness sets in just on 70 m.p.h. in top, giving an initial impression of undergeared fussiness. The average enthusiast will probably forgive such deficiencies since the car is such fun to drive far and fast, but our mythical executive might well want quieter transport for his £982, even though at £92 the extra bits are a bargain.

PRICE: £799 plus £183 2s. 1d. purchase tax equals £982 2s. 1d.
Radio £27 4s. 6d, with tax; total as tested £1,009 6s. 7d.

The back seat gives plenty of head, knee and shoulder room for adults; there is an ashtray in the back of the transmission tunnel console.

Top: Not surprising that the 1600E has a Cortina Lotus air about it—it has the Lotus wide wheels, lowered suspension and matt black grille, plus also a pair of main beam spots.

Above: Despite their mag alloy appearance, the 5½J section wheels are styled in steel; the 1600E comes in four-door form with a thin gold line down the side and an emblem on the rear pillar.

Left: The capacious boot took 10.9 cu. ft. of our test luggage. The complete toolkit can be seen in use—one jack with ratchet spanner, one wheelbrace.

Below: The vestigial toolkit can be clipped to the floor of the boot.

14"×11"×5"

17½"×13"×6"

21"×15"×7"

28"×21"×9"

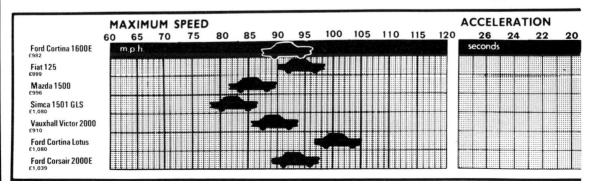

	MAXIMUM SPEED	ACCELERATION
	60 65 70 75 80 85 90 95 100 105 110 115 120	26 24 22 20
Ford Cortina 1600E £982	m.p.h.	seconds
Fiat 125 £999		
Mazda 1500 £996		
Simca 1501 GLS £1,080		
Vauxhall Victor 2000 £910		
Ford Cortina Lotus £1,080		
Ford Corsair 2000E £1,039		

Ford Cortina 1600E *continued*

Performance and economy

Introduced at last year's Paris Show, the 1600E uses a version of the cross-flow bowl-in-piston engine common to the rest of the range; this one is identical with that of the Cortina GT. Compared with the 1600 it has larger valves, a hotter camshaft, a twin-barrel Weber carburetter and a fabricated exhaust manifold. The output is now 88 b.h.p. from 1.6-litres against the original 78 from 1.5 of the earlier G.T.

With full choke it fired first time and pulled smoothly straight away; although it took over two miles for running temperature to appear on the gauge, the choke could be pushed in after little more than a mile. When warm it pulled well from 1,500 r.p.m. but you can't use less than this in top gear (26 m.p.h.) without getting some snatch from the harsh drive line. Above this is a usefully wide torque band and you can use all the revs to advantage, up to the indicated limit of 6,000 r.p.m. Unfortunately, a noticeably harsh period starts at about 4,000 r.p.m. which thus acts as a pottering rev limit; it is really because the engine is initially so unobtrusive that you are the more conscious of the change. This harshness is at its worst between 4,200 and 4,600 r.p.m. but still noticeable beyond although in top gear it gets drowned by wind noise at high speeds. If you are in an over-70 m.p.h. land this might get a little wearisome but the engine is certainly quite happy to maintain as much as a steady 90 m.p.h. (5,200 r.p.m.) if you want to. It is a pity really that the 3.778 final drive of the Cortina Lotus is not offered as an extra as the 3½% gearing increase would put 70 m.p.h. just below the onset of the harshness.

The gearing is just right for maximum speed at 96.3 m.p.h. and the engine pulled an indicated 6,000 r.p.m. on the fastest straight at MIRA (the rev counter being about 250 r.p.m. fast at this

Continued on the next page

Performance

Performance tests carried out by *Motor's* staff at the Motor Industry Research Association proving ground, Lindley.

Test Data: World copyright reserved; no unauthorised reproduction in whole or in part.

Conditions

Weather: Dry but foggy, no wind.
Temperature 30°-32°F. Barometer 29.05 in. Hg.
Surface: Dry concrete and tarmacadam.
Fuel: Premium 98 octane (RM), 4-star rating.

Maximum speeds

	m.p.h.
Mean lap banked circuit	96.2
Best one-way ¼-mile	98.9
3rd gear } at 6,000 r.p.m.	74
2nd gear }	51⅓
1st gear	35

"Maximile" speed: (Timed quarter mile after 1 mile accelerating from rest)

Mean	95.8
Best	96.8

Acceleration times

m.p.h.	sec.
0-30	3.8
0-40	5.7
0-50	8.4
0-60	11.8
0-70	16.2
0-80	23.6
0-90	37.9
Standing quarter mile	18.6

m.p.h.	Top sec.	3rd sec.
10-30	—	7.2
20-40	10.6	6.6
30-50	10.2	6.3
40-60	10.1	6.5
50-70	11.5	8.3
60-80	14.2	
70-90	22.0	

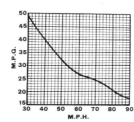

Fuel consumption

Touring (consumption midway between 30 m.p.h. and maximum less 5% allowance for acceleration) . . . . 24.7 m.p.g.
Overall . . . . 23.1 m.p.g.
(=12.2 litres/100 km.)
Total test figure . . . . 1,150 miles
Tank capacity (maker's figure) . . . . . 10 gal.

Brakes

Pedal pressure, deceleration and equivalent stopping distance from 30 m.p.h.

lb.	g	ft.
25	0.33	91
50	0.68	44
70	0.95	31½
Handbrake	0.43	70

Fade test

— 20 stops at ½g deceleration at 1 min. intervals
— from a speed midway between 30 m.p.h. and

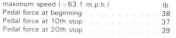

.maximum speed (=63.1 m.p.h.) lb.	
Pedal force at beginning	38
Pedal force at 10th stop	37
Pedal force at 20th stop	39

Steering

	ft.
Turning circle between kerbs:	
Left	27⅓
Right	28⅔
Turns of steering wheel from lock to lock	3.9
Steering wheel deflection for 50 ft. diameter circle	1.05 turns

Clutch

Free pedal movement	= ½ in.
Additional movement to disengage clutch completely	= 3 in.
Maximum pedal load	=22 lb.

Speedometer

Indicated	10	20	30	40	50	60	70	80	90
True	9	20	30	39⅓	49⅓	58⅓	69	79	89

Distance recorder . . . . 1½% fast

Weight

Kerb weight (unladen with fuel for approximately 50 miles) . . . . 18.2 cwt.
Front/rear distribution 55/45
Weight laden as tested . . . . 21.9 cwt.

Parkability

Gap needed to clear a 6ft. wide obstruction parked in front.

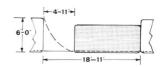

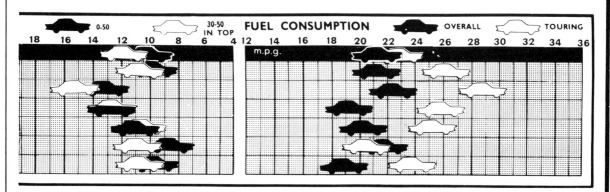

Wooden cappings and facia make the 1600E look quite luxurious inside; reclining seats are standard—they hold well on corners too. Central locker is of useful size.

Ford Cortina 1600E *continued*

speed). This maximum is usefully higher than the 91.5 m.p.h. of our 1963 Cortina GT and very good for a 1.6-litre saloon which, incidentally, has a higher drag factor than the previous Cortina shape. However, the extra power has only just got the better of greater weight and a higher first gear, as witness the 0—60 time of 11.8 s. compared with 12.1 s. for the original 1500GT. These figures certainly confirm the impression of "instant acceleration" you feel when surging past slow traffic in the high second gear.

If you take the 4,000 r.p.m. harshness seriously (and it isn't really that obtrusive) you will probably do most of your motoring on the primary choke of the compound Weber, to the benefit of fuel consumption; although the transition between the chokes is not so easy to feel through the accelerator as it used to be, such motoring should return 25–28 m.p.g. while more spirited driving will drop the figure nearer to our overall 23.1 m.p.g. On a 10-gallon tank this allows only about 200 miles per tankful of the recommended four-star fuel; the engine seemed quite happy on the lower (97 octane) end of this scale.

Transmission

The gearbox is really excellent with unbeatable synchromesh on all four ratios; however fast you push the solid lever through the gate the movement is always smooth and the next gear seems automatically to pick up at exactly the right revs. The ratios aren't particularly close (as in the original Lotus Cortina) but they suit almost any conditions on the road with particularly useful second gear performance up to 50 m.p.h. First gear is good for over 30 m.p.h. but not for a start on a 1-in 3 hill as the light clutch, which juddered slightly when inching forward either when parking or in traffic, just slipped.

There is a little gear whine noticeable in the three indirects but once into top there is no whine at all from either the gearbox or back axle.

Handling and brakes

As well as being lower than on the GT, the front suspension on the 1600E has a zero castor angle which makes the steering feel a little dead, even sticky, in the straight ahead position; once into a

corner though, the self aligning torque of the big India Autobands gives plenty of useful feel and on wet roads you know exactly how much adhesion is left.

With a smaller leather rimmed wheel the steering feels pleasantly direct, just over one turn being needed for a 50 ft. circle; but it also feels a little heavy on tight turns beyond the crossed-arms stage.

The grip on dry roads is very good and the car feels extremely stable when cornering at high speeds; it is even more impressive on slippery surfaces, particularly those wet and greasy ones you find in the farming countryside at this time of year. It will take corners at speeds that you think must provoke a tail slide yet you

Safety check list

Steering assembly	
Steering box position	On bulkhead
Steering column collapsible	No
Steering wheel boss padded	No
Steering wheel dished	Yes

Instrument panel	
Projecting switches	Yes
Sharp cowls	No
Padding	Top and bottom of facia and parcel shelf

Windscreen and visibility	
Screen type	Zone toughened
Pillars padded	Covered
Standard driving mirrors	Interior
Interior mirror framed	Yes
Interior mirror collapsible	Yes
Sun visors	Soft, collapsible

Seats and harness	
Attachment to floor	Runners bolted to floor
Do they tip forward?	No
Head rest attachment points	No
Back of front seats	Padded frame
Safety harness	Lap and diagonal
Harness anchors at back	No

Doors	
Projecting handles	Yes
Anti-burst latches	Yes
Child-proof locks	Yes—on rear doors

come out thinking: "Gosh, I could have gone through that even faster". On public roads, it is usually the driver's nerve, not the tyres' adhesion that sets the limit which makes it all very safe. On wet roads you can produce a final gentle oversteer by using full power in third but you have to try hard in second on dry roads to get the tail going at all, and even then the slight side-step is more or less self-correcting. The behaviour is much the same in the wet as the tail never swings wildly but just floats gently aside and can be held very easily. This is the first test car we have had on India Autobands and they deserve a lot of credit for the good wet roadholding of the 1600E; only when trying very hard at MIRA did they squeal. Radius arms help, too, as there was never any tendency to tramp, even during our standing starts. These used to provoke the most ear-shattering thumps from the back axle on previous GTs but good suspension design has cured this and also improved the handling, while efficient damping keeps the car on an even keel in S bends and there is little roll even on long fast corners. When trying hard and enjoying this sort of fast motoring you tend to forget deficiencies in riding comfort.

The brakes feel pleasantly firm and don't have the oversensitivity of some servo-assisted systems which makes the well placed pedal an ideal leaning post during heel-and-toeing. In our fade test there was no deterioration at all but the watersplash considerably reduced braking efficiency and several stops were needed before this was restored. The rear wheels locked first during our maximum stop and slewed the tail a bit but 0.96g was good on the surface; 0.43g was achieved by the handbrake in a locked rear wheel stop and it could hold the car easily on a 1-in-3 hill.

Continued on the next page

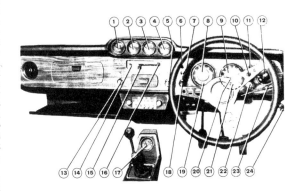

1, ammeter. 2, oil pressure gauge. 3, temperature gauge. 4, fuel gauge. 5, cigar lighter. 6, panel light, 7, LH indicator tell-tale. 8, rev. counter. 9, speedometer. 10, RH indicator tell-tale. 11, light switch. 12, facia vent control. 13, choke. 14, two speed fan. 15, heater direction control. 16, heater temperature. 17, clock. 18, wiper/washer. 19, generator tell-tale. 20, total mileage recorder. 21, main beam tell-tale. 22, ignition/starter key. 23, indicator/flasher/dipper stalk. 24, bonnet release.

Specification

FORD 1600E   FEB 1968   ELS.

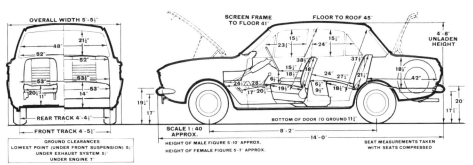

Engine

Cylinders	4
Bore and stroke	81.0 mm. x 77.6 mm.
Cubic capacity	1,599 c.c.
Valves	Pushrod o.h.v.
Compression ratio	9 0:1
Carburetter	Weber 32DFM mechanical compound
Fuel pump	AC mechanical
Oil filter	Fram or Tecalemit full flow
Max. power (net)	88 b.h.p. at 5.400 r.p.m.
Max. torque (net)	96 lb.ft. at 3.600 r.p.m.

Transmission

Clutch	Borg and Beck s.d.p. 7.54 in. dia.
Top gear (s/m)	1.00
3rd gear (s/m)	1.40
2nd gear (s/m)	2.01
1st gear (s/m)	2.97
Reverse	3.32
Final drive	Hypoid bevel 3.91:1
M.p.h. at 1,000 r.p.m. in:—	
Top gear	17.2
3rd gear	12.3
2nd gear	8.6
1st gear	5.8

Chassis

Construction	Unitary

Brakes

Type	Girling disc/drum
Dimensions	Discs 9⅜ in. dia. Drums 9 in. dia.

Friction areas:

Front	20.64 sq.in. of lining operating on 189.5 sq.in. of disc
Rear	48.0 sq.in. of lining operating on 98.8 sq.in. of drum

Suspension and steering

Front	Independent: MacPherson strut with lower wishbone incorporating anti-roll bar; coil springs
Rear	Live axle with leaf springs and upper radius arms
Shock absorbers:	
Front	Telescopic with strut
Rear	Telescopic
Steering gear	Burman recirculating ball
Tyres	India Autoband 165-13
Rim size	5½ J-13

Coachwork and equipment

Starting handle	No
Jack	Screw pillar
Jacking points	Two each side under door sills
Battery	12 volt negative earth. 38 amp hrs. capacity
Number of electrical fuses	None
Indicators	Self-cancelling flashers
Screen wipers	Single speed. self parking
Screen washers	Manual plunger
Sunvisors	Two
Locks:	
With ignition key	Driver's door and boot

Interior heater	Fresh air with cold air facia vents
Extras	Radio
Upholstery	Pvc
Floor covering	Carpet
Alternative body styles	None

Maintenance

Sump	6.2 pints SAE 10W/30
Gearbox	2.1 pints SAE 80 EP
Rear axle	2 pints SAE 90 EP
Steering gear	EP 90
Cooling system	11.4 pints (2 drain taps)
Chassis lubrication	None
Minimum service interval	6.000 miles
Ignition timing	8° b.t.d.c.
Contact breaker gap	0.025 in.
Sparking plug gap	0.023/0.027 in.
Sparking plug type	Autolite AG22A
Tappet clearances (hot)	Inlet 0.012 in. Exhaust 0.022 in.
Valve timing:	
Inlet opens	27° b.t.d.c.
Inlet closes	65° a.b.d.c.
Exhaust opens	65° b.b.d.c.
Exhaust closes	27° a.t.d.c.
Front wheel toe-in	0.12–0.18 in.
Camber angle	1°
Castor angle	0°
King pin inclination	7° 56'
Tyre pressures:	
Front	24 p.s.i.
Rear	24 p.s.i.

Ford Cortina 1600E *continued*

Comfort and controls

Although the Cortina Lotus suspension is fine for earholing in safety you have to accept sacrifices in the ride with what is a fairly conventional suspension design. At town speeds the radial tyes transmit almost every bump as a remote but nevertheless audible thump, bigger disturbances generate other thumps from the rear wheels via the rather rigid radius arms. You feel all these too, although the good seats do a lot to mask them; there is, however, none of the coarse surface road roar that cross ply tyres create.

Out of town at higher speeds the stiffer springing on the 1600E, compared with the 1600, makes the car follow the road contours fairly faithfully giving a restless, if not uncomfortable, ride on all but the smoothest surfaces, though good damping prevents any float.

We all liked the seating position; it is comfortable for all sizes, gives a commanding view over the bonnet and there are no blind spots unless the fixed quarter light gets dirty. The cushion is rather horizontal and therefore lacking in thigh support, but the back rest is well shaped for side location and adjusts through a wide range of angles. The main criticism is that the low steering wheel is too close to the knees of crossed arm twirlers or those who heel and toe.

Once you have adjusted the lap and diagonal seat belt so that the buckle rests on your hip, rather than behind the seat, it is quite easy to fasten; the handbrake gets a little far away when the belt is tight but all other controls are within easy reach; inertia reels are available for those who follow driving test procedure and grab the handbrake at every stop. The back seat (for which there are no belt anchorages) will take three adults fairly comfortably and two very easily with plenty of knee and shoulder room, even with the front seats fully back.

We have already mentioned the engine and wind noise; the latter stems from the door seals and starts as a steady rush from about 40 m.p.h., building up a little as speed increases. If you adjust the radio, a good Ford extra, for comfortable listening at 40 m.p.h. you can't understand speech at 70 m.p.h.; many cars are worse but an E should be better. Improved door seals and a little engine smoothing would make this an effortless 80—90 m.p.h. autobahn cruiser; as it is it may well get tiring with prolonged over-70 use.

Retaining the original Aeroflow system with better facia vent controls, the Cortina equipment is more versatile than the simplified Escort or Zephyr versions. The direction lever gives a degree of volume control if you keep it between "screen" and "off", although the handbook makes no mention of this fact; most people will just divert the greater flow to the screen if their legs are getting too warm and use the fresh air vents as coolers. It is an extremely good system which needs little readjustment with changing road speed and it keeps the windows well demisted. A two-speed booster fan is also fitted.

On the 1600E a pair of Wipac spot lamps supplement the existing lights on main beam to give a simple "four-eyed" conversion; the result is that main beam is so bright and strong that dip is almost yellow by comparison giving the effect of plunging you into relative darkness. The two-speed wipers don't lift off at speed, clean the screen well and sweep right up to the edge of the right hand pillar.

Fittings and furniture

The interior design of the 1600E is identical to that of the GT except for wood cappings all round the waistline and on the facia where the extra thickness is used to recess the two lighting switches, panel and side/head. The other controls are well placed within reach including the combined flasher/dipper/indicator stalk, and the auxiliary instruments mounted on top are easy to glance at. A clock is fitted on the forward end of the gear lever console.

While the car is itself safe to drive by virtue of its swervability, acceleration and brakes, some of the facia and door protrusions look a bit sharp and unlikely to collapse if hit by flying bodies in the second collision.

A further criticism of the door design is that you should be able to unlock your passenger's door first, an elementary courtesy which could perhaps be forgiven if the owner had a cheaper model than the 1600E.

Upholstery in pvc, and carpets, make the 1600E easy to keep clean but the light-coloured seats in our car may well get dirty rather quickly if E stands for Enthusiast. A glove locker is provided in all the Cortinas but only the GT, 1600E and Lotus versions get a useful central locker cum arm rest. Most of the luggage can go in the vast boot which takes 10.9 cu. ft. of our test luggage, possibly a shade less than a GT which doesn't have the 5½J spare wheel (now hidden under a cover).

Accessibility and maintenance

The 1600E has an interior bonnet release, a fact which confused more than one mechanic checking the oil—it's usually the button in the centre of the grille. Once open, the bonnet is propped on a convenient strut and there is plenty of room around the engine for the home mechanic to do most of his own servicing. This is required every 6,000 miles and the schedule is particularly comprehensive, the only additional features which don't need attention every 6,000 miles being a new air cleaner element and the checking of front wheel toe-in. So it is no longer a question of the home mechanic doing the small services between the major ones—they are all major but less frequent. The standard toolkit will be no help at all for this as you still only get wheel changing equipment; this can now be clipped to the floor instead of sliding around.

Maintenance summary

Every 6,000 miles change engine oil and filter, clean air cleaner, check and adjust valve clearances, clean crankcase emission valve, clean oil filler cap, clean fuel filter bowl, lubricate distributor and generator rear bearing, check and adjust distributor points, clean distributor cap and coil, clean and reset plugs, adjust fan belt and tighten generator bolts, check battery level, check radiator level, check washer operation, top-up gearbox and rear axle, check rear spring U-bolts and inserts, check front suspension cross-member bolts and front suspension/steering joint gaiters, check and top-up clutch and brake reservoirs, check pads and brake shoes for wear, inspect brake hoses, top up steering box, check and adjust front wheel bearings, lubricate hand brake cable, door locks, bonnet safety catch and all oil can points, check operation of all controls instruments and lights, check seat belts for security and wear, road test car and adjust carburetter and ignition if necessary.

Every 18,000 miles renew air cleaner, check front wheel toe-in, repack and adjust front wheel bearings.

Every 36,000 miles renew all brake seals hydraulic fluid and flexible brake hoses.

1, battery. 2, brake fluid reservoir. 3, starter solenoid. 4, oil filler cap. 5, radiator cap. 6, dipstick. 7, junction box. 8, washer reservoir.

MAKE: Ford. **MODEL:** 1600E. **MAKERS:** Ford Motor Company Ltd., Dagenham, Essex.

OWNER'S VIEW

John Danvers, 1600E owner and enthusiast, interviews Ray Sanby, Chairman of the Ford Cortina 1600E Owners' Club. Ray lives in Sheffield, South Yorkshire.

JD: Why are you so interested in the 1600E?
RS: I can't pin it down to one particular thing. Basically the whole car just fits with the way I like to drive – that is, in style and in comfort and with enough power to suit the prevailing traffic conditions.
JD: When and why did you buy your 1600E?
RS: I bought it six years ago. It was advertised simply as a Cortina E and was one of several vehicles I went to look at that evening. When the chap opened the garage door I thought 'Ye gods, what's that?', and after I'd given it a quick going over I realised it was something more than I'd bargained for, and certainly better value than the other cars I'd seen. It just looked right and drove beautifully!
JD: What condition was it in?
RS: On the whole it was quite sound, although the rear wheel arches were just beginning to deteriorate. They're a common problem and one of the best mud traps designed by Ford – they made them even bigger on the Mk IV and Mk V!
JD: Have you done any restoration work on the car?
RS: I had to replace every single

panel forward of the front bulkhead in 1978 thanks to a drunken driver. While those repairs were being done I also had both sills and the rear offside wing replaced at the same time, followed by a complete respray.
JD: Have you experienced difficulty in obtaining any parts?
RS: Oh certainly, everybody does – although a lot of the problems are caused by parts counter staff at dealers. As soon as you mention the 1600E you get the usual sharp intake of breath, accompanied by the 'it will take at least three months to get it' routine. It would help tremendously if they would remember that a considerable number of the 1600E's mechanical and body parts are also common to other cars in the Mk II range. For the record though, inner wings and interior trim are particularly difficult to obtain at the moment.
JD: How would you describe the 1600E's handling and performance?
RS: Both are good for a car of its weight. When nearly a ton of motor car goes round a corner, tremendous lateral forces come into play, so the E's suspension has to work – otherwise you'd get the back end breaking away. The car always gives you plenty of warning and in that respect is very safe to fling about. There are, of course, many cars around nowadays which in standard form can out-perform the 1600E, but you'll find that most of them are somewhat lighter – so the E's performance even by today's standards is still more than acceptable.
JD: Is your car in everyday use – and is it practical in today's conditions?
RS: I use it regularly at the moment, but I intend to take it off the road within the next few months for a total restoration. I find the running costs slightly higher than average, but they're more than tolerable in view of the enjoyment I get.
JD: Has your car won any prizes in concours or similar events?

RS: No, I've never entered it and have no particular desire to do so.
JD: How would you summarize the benefits of the 1600E Owner's Club for its members?
RS: The social side of the Club is very rewarding – especially the meetings. Go to any of the Club's events – a local branch meeting for example, or the annual National Rally – and you'll find members exchanging views and comparing notes about their cars. It's amazing the amount of information that is circulated between people who have a common interest – information which we try to capture in our quarterly magazine and which enables members not only to keep their running and general maintenance costs to a minimum, but which, in the long run, we hope will help them to keep their 1600Es on the road for as long as possible.
JD: What advice would you give to potential owners of the 1600E?
RS: As with any older vehicle, just be very, very careful when looking the car over – be sure to check the body thoroughly as Cortinas can sometimes rust in a number of not so obvious places. And if considering a major restoration make sure the parts are available *before* dismantling the car!
JD: And finally, how would you sum up the enjoyment you get from your 1600E?
RS: I've driven most types of car, and yet I still find the 1600E to be one of the best all-rounders in terms of styling and performance. Ford got it right, and there's not a lot more I can say!

John Danvers interviews Alan Gudgeon, a driver of long experience and a 1600E Owners' Club member. Alan lives in Leicester.

JD: When did you become interested in the 1600E?
AG: I saw my first 1600E in 1968. It had just been delivered to the owner of my local body repair shop and was one of the first 1600Es in the area. I recall that people

actually came from miles around just to look at it! I was driving a 1600 GT at the time, and although I knew the two cars were almost identical mechanically, the E just *looked* different. The Rostyle wheels and lowered suspension gave the car a definitely more sporty, yet business-like appearance. On reflection I suppose it was these two features, along with the refined interior, that really won me over. I promised myself there and then that I'd own a 1600E eventually.

JD: When did you buy your 1600E?

AG: In 1971. It was first registered in April 1969 and had clocked around 24 000 miles when I got it.

JD: What condition was it in?

AG: Apart from an infuriating squeak in the boot it was in really excellent condition – both mechanically and bodily.

JD: Has it needed any repair or restoration work since?

AG: Initially some repair work, if you can call it that, but not, I hasten to add, through any fault of my own. I had to replace the radio and all five Rostyle wheels when they were stolen in 1974. The police eventually found the car half a mile away and amazingly enough the wooden trim and centre console hadn't been touched! The first real repair session came as the result of an accident in 1977 when the front and rear offside doors were badly damaged. It was at that stage that I decided not just to repair the car but to restore it completely, and since then I've replaced the aforementioned doors, the front and rear wings, the engine, the carburettor, the front struts, the rear dampers, and the rear springs, along with a host of ancillary components.

JD: Have you experienced difficulty in obtaining any parts?

AG: Only recently, I had to wait nearly four months for the correct speedometer cable. Soft trim is particularly difficult to come by should you be unfortunate enough to need it.

JD: How do you rate the 1600E's

performance and handling?

AG: Very good indeed. I've always made full use of the gears – especially third which I find particularly exhilarating. Many's the time I've been pulled out of a potentially dangerous traffic situation by the E's third gear acceleration and positive handling. To the uninitiated, the ride and steering would feel hard and heavy respectively, but they're things you get used to quickly, and are very much part and parcel of the car's driveability.

JD: Is your car in everyday use?

AG: Yes – for getting to and from work as well as for pleasure. In fact up until two years ago it was my full time business transport as well, and in one year alone I clocked up nearly 20 000 miles on company business. I was offered a company car but turned it down – under no circumstances was I going back to an *ordinary* car again!

JD: Has your car won any prizes in concours or similar events?

AG: No – I've never entered it. I tend to shy away from public events of that type, but I doubt whether anyone is prouder of their car than I am of mine.

JD: You're a member of the 1600E Owners' Club – do you find membership of the Club useful?

AG: I've never really taken full advantage of the Club's services, and just prefer to remain on the periphery of all the activity. I look forward to receiving the Club's

quarterly magazine and reading about other E owners and their experiences, although I must admit I sometimes find the technical information beyond my mechanical know-how. The Club has certainly stimulated a lot of interest in the 1600E and has made many owners aware of the need to preserve their cars instead of driving them into obscurity. Now there must be over a thousand 1600Es in reasonable-to-A1 condition that might not have been so, had the Club not existed.

JD: And finally, how would you sum up the enjoyment you get from your 1600E?

AG: I love driving it – it's as simple as that. In addition to providing my everyday transport and, at one time, playing an important role in earning my living, my E has also given countless hours of pleasure to me and my family.

I just couldn't imagine myself behind the wheel of any other car!

BUYING

The choice of 1600Es, available for purchase and preservation in the 1980s, varies widely from country to country. Clearly the UK enthusiast will have the most scope, for 11,371 of the original type and 28,693 of the 'face-lift' models were originally sold in the domestic market. Some 1600Es survive in Ford's traditional export markets, and some (including the rare left-hand drive derivatives) in Western Europe, but there are very few indeed in North America, or further afield. Apart from the two-doors in Europe, all 1600Es which are genuine are four-door saloons.

Genuine? I use the word advisedly, simply because it is possible to produce a passable '1600E' copy from the bare bones of a suitable GT, if the operator is determined, or, perhaps, dishonest, enough. My first advice, therefore, to all potential 1600E buyers, is to make sure the chassis plate, and all the trim and decorative detail makes sense. The chassis series, incidentally, should be 3036E if the car is right-hand drive, and 3037E if left-hand drive.

So, what is available? The answer is — far fewer than the original production statistics might suggest. In the early and mid 1970s many 1600Es were neglected, sold on, allowed to rust away, and eventually abandoned by their 'nth' owners, so that by the time interest and enthusiasm in the 1600E began to glow again, the stock of good examples had been sadly depleted.

Which 1600Es are best? To misquote George Orwell — all 1600Es are equal, but some are more equal than others. Basically, all 1600Es were built with the same type of 'chassis', suspension, and performance, and the same type of accommodation and equipment. There is no doubt in my mind, however, that the four-door car was better than the two-door car in terms of general convenience (if you have a choice — which you don't have in the UK), and that a late-model 'face-lift' car built in 1969 or 1970 has the best instrument layout, the best gearbox, and the nicest interior trim. Statistically, indeed, more 'face-lift' cars survive, because there were many more of them, and they have had less time in which to rust away.

The value of a 1600E slumped predictably in the mid 1970s, so that a good, sound, example could be bought for a mere £500 or so, but this began to rise from 1978 onwards, and by the early 1980s a very good example might command £1,500 and a truly outstanding 'concours' 1600E up to £2,000. Since then values, if anything, have trended slightly downwards again.

I must emphasise, of course, that under the skin the 1600E was no more complex, and no better preserved on assembly, than any other Ford of the late 1960s, which means that there are several areas in which deterioration can, and often has, become obvious. Body shells can rust, suspensions and transmissions can wear out. That, however, is the bad news. The good news is that Ford, or their dealers, can still supply many mechanical and some body parts for the restoration or rebuilding of these cars, so if you find a badly knocked about example, with a modicum of dedication it should be possible to see it put back into A1 condition.

Mechanically, the 'what to look for' points are concentrated in the steering gear and suspension bushes, for the engines and the transmissions should last for a very long time if they have regularly been maintained. In regard to engines, as long as they do not suffer from worn pistons, and valve gear, or use too much oil, they should be ready to provide a spirited performance, but look for correct timing and carburettor adjustments, and at the general condition of the fabricated exhaust manifold.

A noisy, clonky, rear axle will tell its own story (parts to rebuild are available), as will a sloppy gearbox linkage, or a lack of synchromesh, particularly on first or second gears. In general, however, the transmission lasts as long as the engine before a major rebuild is necessary — probably in excess of 80,000 miles.

You may not like it that way, but the suspension should feel firm, shading on the harsh on some surfaces. If not, either the dampers are deteriorating, or non-standard components have been fitted in the past. Beware of any 1600E which does not sit low to the road (lower, anyway, than most Mk II Cortinas), or one that does not have Rostyle wheels, which are no longer made. The most important suspension wear points are the ball joints at the bottom of MacPherson struts, bushes in track control arms, and for mounting anti-roll bars, and bushes in the rear suspension radius arms, which may 'clonk' alarmingly. You can get replacements for all these parts.

The steering on 1600Es is by recirculating ball, and this may have worn, and be sloppy. Wear can be taken up in the box, if you must, and new bushes and joints for the rest of the linkage are also available.

By modern standards, the disc front/drum rear braking system is very simple, and replacement parts from Girling are all available.

Rear drum brakes are self-adjusting, a feature which has caused problems in the past, and be sure that the handbrake mechanism (particularly the early 'under-facia' type) is in a reasonable state. A brake servo was not standard, but many 1600Es had them fitted as an option. I think a servo is desirable, if it's working well.

I don't recommend having a 1600E with larger-section, non-standard tyres – the steering is heavy enough at low speeds as it is. If the wheels and tyres of a 1600E are in good condition, and the correct type, that is a bonus for the purchaser. Incidentally, be sure that the correct type of steering wheel, with polished alloy spokes, and padded 'leather' rim, is still fitted, complete with a 'Cortina' motif in the centre.

Look for three major features in the bodywork of a 1600E you might consider buying – the general incidence of rust, the quality of the paintwork (especially metallic) and the completeness of the furniture and fittings.

Cortina bodies rust, I'm afraid – did you expect anything else? Look, in particular, around the front suspension MacPherson strut towers (a high-stress area), near the bonnet hinge supports, behind the headlamps, the joints of inner wheel arches with other body panels (and the bulkhead), the sills under the doors, the lower rear wings behind the wheels, and the rear wheel arches. Treat any sign of water leakage to the boot area with great suspicion.

Have a good look for rust around the lower front panel, the front edge of the bonnet, the rear edge of the boot lid, and the bottom of doors, along the 'chassis legs', around the rear spring hangers, and where the front cross-member bolts up to the underbody. Other rust 'starters' are the base of the screen pillars, and the joint between roof and rear wings. When poking around underneath the car, in a ramp inspection (you wouldn't

buy a unit-construction car without one, would you?), make sure the seat mountings, gearbox fixings, handbrake hook up, and brackets for the exhaust system are all present, and in good shape. Look, too, at the condition of the radius arm brackets on the under side of the floor pan.

The paint may be in a terrible state, particularly if it is one of the metallic types Ford were promoting so hard at the time. Some of these shades, such as Silver Fox and Blue Mink, seemed to peel off too easily. These days it should be possible to get modern equivalents which adhere better, particularly if pre-paint preparation has been good.

It is very important that the equipment of a 1600E should be complete, and preferably that the woodwork (facia, and door cappings) should be in a good condition. Soft trim and special fittings like these go 'Out-of-Stock' first once a model is obsolete – and don't forget that even the youngest 1600E will be 15 years old in 1985. Wood, of course, can be restored, or re-veneered, but it will be almost impossible to match the pattern of the original.

The seat covers, and styles, too, are difficult to duplicate if you decide to restore a scruffy 1600E – it is always better to persevere in your search for a well-kept example in the first place. Be sure, too, that the car you inspect really does have 1600E seats, instruments, and other fittings, by the way – it is all too easy for a car to have become hybridized over the years, especially in the mid-1970s when all an owner wanted was to keep his car on the road, not necessarily in an original state.

My experience is that items which may be missing, 'modified',

or replaced by non-standard items include the radio and the correct type of carpets or seats. In the boot, for example, be sure that there is carpet on the floor, and a cover for the spare wheel. Outside the car, it is all too easy for one or both auxiliary driving lamps (front), or under-bumper reverse lamps (rear) to have gone missing, even – I'm afraid – for the correct 1600E badge to be an absentee.

The question of correct grilles is vexed – according to my information all 1600Es of whatever age should have all-black grilles, but I have also seen a number of 'face-lift' cars with the more ornate grille normally found on bread-and-butter Cortina MkIIs. I have to say that I prefer the all-black variety, which enhances the 'executive' image of the car.

If you do buy a 1600E, incidentally, I recommend that you have it thief-proofed, and that at the same time you invest in a set of locking wheel nuts to prevent the theft of those splendid wheels, which seem to be very attractive to the light-fingered fraternity, whether amateur or professional!

1600Es, though not widely available, are usually advertised for sale in the 'classic' or 'enthusiast' motoring magazines, and of course there is a steady and honest market within the 1600E enthusiast clubs themselves. A 1600E is rarely found in a normal dealer showroom these days.

CLUBS, SPECIALISTS & BOOKS

Clubs

Whether your interests lie in basic maintenance or ultimately in major restoration, or you simply wish to meet fellow enthusiasts in order to broaden your knowledge of a particular model, joining the relevant one-make owners' club is always to be recommended.

As far as the 1600E is concerned, the largest club to join is **The Ford Cortina 1600E Owners' Club,** (National 1600E Owners' Club and Ford 1600E Club are other titles by which it has also been known).

The Club was established in 1976 and was run for local enthusiasts in the Leicester and Manchester areas at first. During the following twelve months it became apparent from countrywide enquiries that some form of national club was required, and in the summer of 1977 the Club was reorganised into its present form. It has since grown rapidly and, at the time of writing, had approximately 1500 members registered throughout the UK and overseas. The Club is recognised by the Ford Motor Company as the official 1600E Owners' Club.

There are currently 18 branches of the Club, with others under development, in various areas of the UK, which enable the more active members to meet regularly and thus gain first-hand advice and assistance with their 1600Es whilst simultaneously stimulating their interests in both car and Club. These branches organize their own outings and meetings and also combine to stage larger area rallies at varying locations in the summer months.

A National Rally is held annually over a weekend period at a suitable venue to cater for the needs of the member and his family, and those attending can enjoy film shows, disco and social evening on the Saturday, with concours and class car competitions, autojumble and full supporting programme on the Sunday.

The Club produces an informative quarterly magazine – *The Executive* – which contains a wealth of information including regular articles, hints and tips, details of activities, club mart and other items of special interest to the 1600E owner. Individual branches provide regular newsletters thus keeping their members in touch with news aimed at a more local level.

With some spares becoming unobtainable, particularly body panels, the Club is arranging for manufacturers to produce these items for sale to members. Additionally, limited but progressive bulk purchase of original manufacturers' spares is being made for resale to members at favourable rates.

Membership is open to all 1600E *owners,* and enquiries should be addressed to the Secretary: Alan Clarke, 22 Stonehurst Road, Braunstone, Leicester.

Since September 1982, however, there has been an alternative club with a very similar name: **The Ford Cortina 1600E Enthusiast's Club.** Its aims and ambitions are virtually the same, but naturally the officers and the organisation are entirely different. Membership was approaching 300 by the end of 1983. One can become a full or associate member by contacting the Secretary: Peter Underwood, 54 Fairfield Drive, Dorking, Surrey RH4 1JH. Tel: 0306-886193.

Specialists

Although no 1600E 'specialists' as such have so far appeared, there certainly isn't any shortage of expertise when it comes to 1600E maintenance and repair. Indeed, any reputable garage/body shop which can obtain spares effectively should be quite capable of undertaking the majority of, if not all, mechanical and structural repairs on the model– of course the wise owner will seek recommendations from fellow owners before deciding to whom or where to allocate the job.

In addition to the existing network of Ford dealers the following specialist suppliers are known to cater for 1600E enthusiasts – usually as part of a more general service to car owners:-

Auto-Trim, Unit 2, Wesley Street, Leicester. Tel: Leicester (0533) 64112.

Full retrimming service, repairs to seats, carpets, etc.

Ford 50 Spares, 69 Jolliffe Road, Poole, Dorset. Tel: Poole (0202) 679258.

Various body panels, mechanical spares, suspension and steering components. Stock range under constant review.

Kent Restoration Services, 5 Bank House, The Broadway, Sheerness, Kent. Tel. Minster (0795) 873466.

Stripping and re-finishing of wooden facias and door cappings.

L.M.C. Manufacturing Ltd,
Quartermaster Road, West Wilts
Trading Estate, Westbury,
Wiltshire. Tel: Westbury (0373)
865088
     Manufacturers and suppliers
of panels and repair sections.

Newford Parts Centre, Fishwick
Lane, Higher Wheelton, Nr.
Chorley, Lancs. Tel: Brinscall
(0254) 830343.
     Large stocks of mechanical
components and body panels for
older Fords, including the Mk II
Cortina. Stock range under
constant review.

Tollpower Ltd, (Trading as J.B.W.),
Wedgnock Lane, Wedgnock
Industrial Estate, Warwick. Tel:
Warwick (0926) 496131.
     Rostyle wheels and
associated accessories.

Withers of Winsford Ltd,
Smokehall Lane, Wharton,
Winsford, Cheshire. Tel: Winsford
(06065) 4422.
     New and used parts, wooden
trim, Rostyle wheels, some body
panels.

Books

This is the first book to be
published about the 1600E alone,
although the following include
information on the type:

**Cortina Mk II Owner's Workshop
Manual:** A complete guide to all
mechanical repairs and overhaul
tasks on all Mk II models (except
Lotus).Published by Haynes.

**Cortina Mk I and Mk II Owner's
Handbook:** An easy-to-follow yet
thorough guide to routine
maintenance and servicing on all
Cortina models 1962 to 1970
(except Lotus versions). Published
by Haynes.

"The Sporting Fords, Volume 1:
Cortinas – a collectors guide" by
Graham Robson: A factual survey
of the high performance, sporting
and executive Cortinas of 1963 to
1970. Published by Motor Racing
Publications.

PHOTO GALLERY

1

2

3

1.   1600Es as far as the eye can see – at an early 1980s' concours run by the 1600E Owners' Club. The car in the right foreground has non-standard quarter bumpers and auxiliary driving lamps.

2.   This massive line up of 1600Es at an Owners' Club meeting shows the great enthusiasm which exists for these series-production Ford 'classics'.

3.   The 1967-68 1600Es had an 'office' like this, where the auxiliary instruments were high on the crash roll. This is a 1980s' picture of a preserved car, and the radio installation is a modern type.

4

5

4. The 1969 model 'face-lift' 1600E had an altogether more integrated instrument layout. The radio installation was in the top of the centre console, as seen here. Keen comparison with picture (3) shows the different gear lever 'gate' markings for the latest single-rail gearbox introduced at this time. The alloy-spoked steering wheel was the same on both types. This car, by the way, has more than 70,000 miles on the speedometer!

5. Factory fresh, with polished woodwork, and uncrushed seating. In those days, of course, static safety belts with floppy inner ends were provided. That was a very useful cubby box between the seats. The handbrake on the original cars was alongside the steering column, under the facia.

6. From the beginning of the 1969 model year, not only was the facia layout of the 1600E revised, but there was a new full-length centre console, no cubby box, the single-rail gearbox, and the handbrake was placed between the seats.

7. Variation on a theme – this being a left-hand drive 1970-model 1600E, incorporating a new type of 'safety' steering wheel required by some markets. There was no radio fitted to this car either.

6

7

8

9

8.   Well-kept wood shines ... and shines. This car was 15 years old, but well-loved, when photographed at an Owners' Club meeting.

9.   The vinyl seats of the 1600E can take a great deal of punishment, and always come up well if restored carefully, as this shot of a 15-year-old car confirms.

10.   Close up of the 'safety' steering wheel, with metal 'collapsible can' below the wheel itself, on this left-hand drive 1600E pictured at Ford at the start of the 1969 model year run.

11.   The normal alloy-spoked wheel was very neat on 1600Es, and the gear lever knob was very close to it. In those days, one steering column stalk sufficed to operate the indicators, dip or flash the lights, and sound the horn. Ignition key operation was on the facia panel too, not on the steering column.

10

11

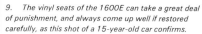

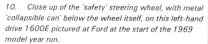

12

13

14

12. *Detail of the neatly integrated centre console on 'face-lift' 1600Es. This is a modern picture, which explains the use of non-standard switches ahead of the gear lever, but the Radiomobile is the type which Ford would have fitted.*

13. *Ford provided an advanced heating and ventilation system on 1600Es – indeed, on all Cortinas, years before their opposition caught up, with volumes of cool air available through the 'eyeball' vents. There was also a very useful parcel shelf.*

14. *The problem with restoring a neglected 1600E is that the door trim panels must look like this – complete with welded pattern details. Notice the shape, fit and finish of the wooden capping-strips to these front doors.*

15. *The seats on 1969 and 1970 1600Es had perforated vinyl facings, which are still available, and should not be abandoned, unless the owner does not think originality is important.*

15

16. Rear door trim and finish details of the 1600E, complete with welded-panel finish, and wooden capping-strips. There is an extra, non-standard, protective piece of plastic on the door shut face of this preserved car.

17. and 18. When Ford introduced the 1969-model 1600E, they produced this new style of rear seat. What's that, you'd like it with an occupant to give it scale? OK then ...

19. When Ford announced the new Bowl-in-Piston engine in 1967, this was the GT specification used in the Cortina GT and the 1600E. The air cleaner has been removed from the carburettor, of course, in this shot.

16

17

18

19

20. No factory-built 1600E ever looked as good as
this! Naturally it is a concours winning example – over-
restored, in the author's opinion.

21 & 22. Two shots of the same nicely-preserved
1600E, at 15 years old, in good up-to-standard
condition. Note the typically-untidy Ford system of
plumbing and wiring from this period, the '1600GT'
label on the rocker cover, the smooth shape of the
exhaust manifold, and the space around the engine
which allows easy maintenance.

20

21

22

23

24

23.   Surprisingly, there was never any plug overheating problem on the Bowl-in-Piston 1600E engines, though I have to admit that they look to be very close indeed to the exhaust ports and manifold.

24.   Selmar car alarm is a sensible extra fitted by this 1600E owner, but the engine bay is otherwise in standard, very clean, condition.

25.   For the first year only (1968 model year), Cortina 1600Es had this type of gearbox; it was replaced by the single-rail selector layout for 1969.

25

26

27

26 & 27. What's so special about a boot lid recess? ... It's where the 1600E's simple jack fits, that's what.

28. Ford included this sticker under the bonnet to provide DIY owners with service information for 1600Es.

29. The very simple three-bolt fixing of the MacPherson strut (front suspension spring/damper unit) to the inner wheel arch – a classic 'what to look for' place in a neglected, rusty, 1600E. But this car is in very good shape indeed.

RECOMMENDED ENGINE ADJUSTMENTS AT MAJOR SERVICE INTERVALS

SPARK PLUGS	VALVE CLEARANCES	
	SET DYNAMICALLY IN PREFERENCE	HOT & COLD
AUTOLITE POWERTIP AG22	EXHAUST	.022 INS 0.56 MM
.023 INS 0.6 MM	INLET	.012 INS 0.30 MM

DISTRIBUTOR
CYLINDER FIRING ORDER 1 2 4 3

LIGHTLY OIL FELT PAD

cam lubrication USE GREASE ONLY (Lithium base)

.025 INS 0.64MM

IGNITION TIMING (BTDC)	
ENGINE DISPLACEMENT	AT IDLE SPEED (700 RPM)
1300CC GT	10° USING 97 OCTANE FUEL
1600CC GT	8° USING 97 OCTANE FUEL
For static setting deduct 4° from above figures	

FoMoCo   2737E 6B315-A

28

29

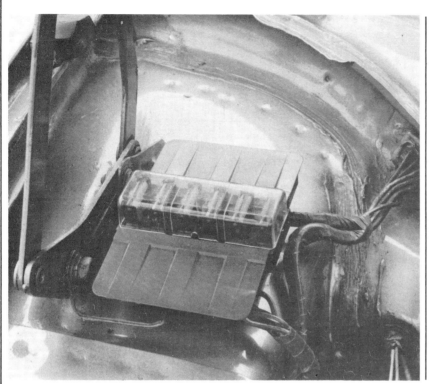

30

30. 1600E fuses were positioned on a platform close to the bonnet hinge on the right side of the engine bay, and were protected by a clear plastic cover.

31. 1600E over-riders, where fitted, were rubber faced. The locking filler cap was a dealer-supplied accessory.

32. The 'official' factory driving lamp for the 1600E was this Wipac unit, complete with vertically mounted bulb, and shallow bowl. Frankly, it was not so much powerful, as easily installed.

33. The 'badge' on the rear quarters of 1600Es said nothing, and denoted nothing, but was an ever present part of the specification. Every preserved 1600E should have them on both sides.

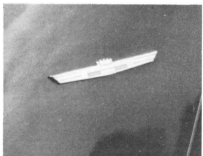

33

31

32

34

35

36

37

34. The only '1600E' badge was on the boot lid, under the 'Cortina' script which appeared on all cars of this family. E for what? Executive was the description most usually applied.

35. Face-lift 1600Es built from the autumn of 1968 onwards had a black-painted rear panel. The owner of this preserved car has ensured even that the screwdriver slot of the right-side number plate fixing is in the ideal alignment!

36. Cortina 1600Es had wide-tread tyres, and a hunkered-down stance, plus extra driving lamps. Overriders were extras, fitted to many cars.

37. Sidelamps and direction indicators were combined behind the same lens on 1600Es, and were neatly incorporated into the outer extremities of the grille.

38.   Neat and simple bonnet release button, incorporated into the front centre of the grille style on 1968-model Cortinas, including the 1600E.

39.   On 1600Es, as on other Mk II Cortinas, the door locks were placed immediately under the door handles themselves, which helped protect them from water entry, and icing up in the winter.

40.   On this particular 1600E, the proud owner has also fitted a burglar alarm, whose actuating key is down near the base of the driver's door.

41.   If a Mk II Cortina body shell is going to rot, one obvious place to look is at the junction of the body sills with the rear wheel arches; the process has started on this car, and should be stopped without delay.

38

39

40

41

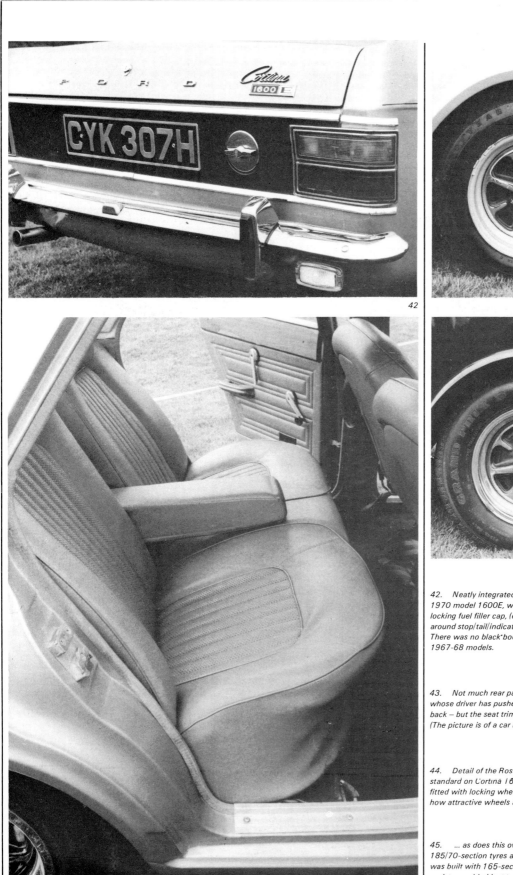

42

45

42. Neatly integrated styling of the rear corner of a 1970 model 1600E, with reversing lamps, (extra) locking fuel filler cap, (extra) over-riders and the wrap-around stop/tail/indicator assemblies used throughout. There was no black body paint across the tail of 1967-68 models.

43. Not much rear passenger leg room in the 1600E, whose driver has pushed the front seats all the way back – but the seat trim is still in excellent condition. (The picture is of a car more than 10 years old.)

44. Detail of the Rostyle wheel which was always standard on Cortina 1600Es. This car has also been fitted with locking wheel nuts by an owner who knows how attractive wheels are to thieves ...

45. ... as does this owner. Strictly speaking, the 185/70-section tyres are too fat for a 1600E, which was built with 165-section tyres when new, but only the purists would object to this today.

43

46

47

48

49. A near relative of the 1600E in many respects was the Mk II Lotus-Cortina, announced in March 1967, half a year before the 1600E. The Lotus Cortina, however, used a two-door saloon style, had pressed-steel wheels, and the famous twin overhead camshaft Lotus-Ford engine.

47. The Mk II Lotus-Cortina used suspension which was basically transferred to the 1600E when it was announced, but did not use the special Rostyle wheels, and had a lot more power (109 bhp vs. 88 bhp).

48. Similar, but different – the Mk II Lotus Cortina of 1970 used the same basic facia/control layout as the 1600E, even down to the 'safety' steering wheel on this left-hand-drive model, but did not have a wooden facia panel, or wood cappings to the doors.

49. Hundreds of Cortina Savages were made by Jeff Uren's 'Race Proved' concern. These were basically converted 1600Es, with 3-litre 'Essex' vee-6 engines ...

CYK 307H

52

MOV 474F

53

50. ... and they were badged accordingly.

51. The facelift Cortinas for 1969 had the FORD name spelled out on the bonnet's nose. Extra grille brightwork on this car was non-standard ...

52. ... which makes this 1600E the real thing, for it has an all-black grille, and the 'Mk II' bonnet and lettering. Ah well ...

53 & 54. A study in tails on 1600Es. MOV 474F is a 1967-68 1600E, where there was no distinctive decoration between the tail lamps. CYK 307H is a face-lift 1600E, complete with black panel across the tail between the lamp clusters.

50

51

CYK 307H

54

55

55.   Nose and tail detail of the face-lift model for 1969, showing the slightly more ornate front grille (on a GT, not a 1600E), and the distinctive tail on the 1600E.

56 & 57.   Two views of the rare export-only two-door 1600E, introduced for the 1969 model year. More than 2000 were made, but none officially went to British buyers. There were, however, important detail differences – such as the lack of decoration on the flanks, the ornate radiator grille, and lack of black body paint across the tail. The steering wheel, too, was of the added 'safety' variety.

56

57

58

58 & 59. One of the very first 1600Es, pictured in the Ford studios at South Ockendon in the summer of 1967, which gives a good idea of the detail fittings which should be fitted on surviving cars.

60, 61 & 62. One of the very first 1600Es on location for Ford's photographic department in the summer of 1967. It was bright red, with chrome-plated Rostyle wheels. The volume of pictures in the Ford archive for this session suggests that everyone enjoyed themselves on this occasion.

59

60

61

62

63

64

63. From this angle, a 1600E looks very purposeful indeed. For a 15-year-old car (when photographed), it looks modern, and very effective indeed.

64. The 'facelift' 1600E, for 1969, complete with FORD lettering on the bonnet, but no over-riders on the standard car.

65. The 1970 model 1600E had this type of detail rear style.

65

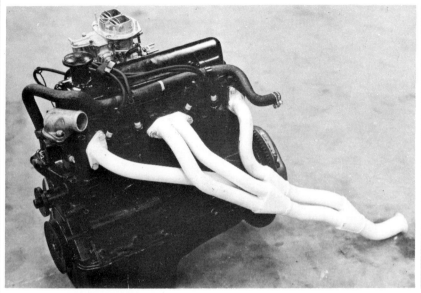

66. The cross-flow 1600GT engine on the workshop floor, ready for installation in a GT, or a 1600E, showing off its particularly efficient exhaust system.

67. The 'E' which preceded the 1600E, and which persuaded Ford to repeat the trick, was the Corsair 2000E, launched in January 1967. In this case, the special touches included the vinyl roof, special wheels and (hidden) more power and better gearbox ratios,

68. Belatedly. Ford tried to follow-up the 1600E's success with the 2000E shown here, but this Mk III Cortina-based car did not arrive until 1973, and lacked the character of the 1600E.

69. The facia style of the Mk III 2000E was smart enough, and had some 1600E-like touches, but that steering wheel was truly awful and somehow the car never had the same sort of sporty quality.

66

67

68

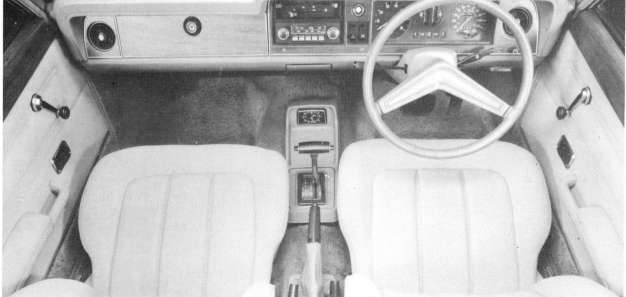

69

C1

C2

C3

C1. The sumptuously furnished interior of the original 1600E of 1967, complete with auxiliary instruments high on the facia layout ...

C2. ... compared with the revised facia style of the 1969 model introduced in the autumn in 1968.

C3. 1600E at twilight, pre-announcement in 1967. Or is it the morning after the night before?

C4. The 1600E's Rostyle wheels added extra class to a well equipped car.

C5. That was real polished tree wood – none of your nasty synthetic stuff – on the facia of the 1600E. They don't make them like that any more ...

C6. This low level shot emphasises the squat stance of the 1600E, and its wide tyres.

C4

C5

C6

C7. A typically 'moody' shot from Ford's studio, before the launch of the 1600E in its definitive form.

C8. There was not a lot to distinguish the 1600E from the four-door GT, except for the wheels, the badging and the extra driving lamps.

C7

C8

C9. Another Ford studio shot of an early 1600E, before over-riders were fitted.

C10. No name, no letters, nothing – just motifs on the rear quarter panels behind the doors, helped identify the 1600E from other Cortinas. Red, white and blue – for British-made?

C11. The original 1600E had a standard body-colour tail, like this pre-production car of 1967 ...

C12

C12. ... but after the face lift of October 1968, there was a black panel across the tail.

C13. The 'face lift' 1600Es (October 1968 onwards) could be distinguished in several ways, one being that the letters 'FORD' were picked out on the bonnet.

C14. Side view of a 1969 model 1600E. Note lack of Ford roundel on front wings.

C13

C14

C15

C16

C15. The G-Registration, and the 'FORD' letters on the bonnet identify this 1600E as a 1969 'face-lift' model.

C16. Photographed in 1983, this 1969-70 1600E was still in magnificent condition. The wing mirrors and the auxiliary lamps below the bumper were added after delivery.

C17

C18

C17. The house (Stanford Hall, near Rugby) is classically styled. Does the green 1969-70 1600E qualify for this status too?

C18. This 1600E was 13 years old when photographed especially for this book and still looked at least as good as new. The wing mirrors were not standard on Dagenham-built cars.

C19

C20

C19. Inviting rear seats of the 'face-lift' 1600E, complete with fold-down arm-rest, though there is no more leg room than you'd expect from a 14 foot long car.

C20. Good quality wood for door-cappings, plushy and comfortable rear seats, and adequate foot space in the back seats of the 1600E. All UK-market 1600Es were four-door saloons, like this example, though there was also a rare two-door model for some export territories.